ABOUT THE AUTHOR

John Seddon is an occupational psychologist, researcher, lecturer and Managing Director of Vanguard Consulting. A leading authority on managing change in organisations, he describes his work as a combination of systems thinking — how the work works — and intervention theory — how to change it.

John is the author of a series of guides and manuals — for an up-to-date list see his website, www.lean-service.com — and has a reputation for being an entertaining and controversial speaker on management and organisations.

THE CASE AGAINST
ISO 9000

John Seddon

Oak Tree Press
Dublin

Oak Tree Press
Merrion Building
Lower Merrion Street
Dublin 2, Ireland
www.oaktreepress.com

A catalogue record of this book is
available from the British Library.

ISBN 1-86076 173-6

Printed in the Republic of Ireland by Colour Books Ltd.

CONTENTS

PREFACE

Since the publication of the first edition of this book in 1997, the growth of ISO 9000 registrations has continued although not perhaps at the pace that many commentators expected. From 102,000 registrations worldwide in 1997, we have now reached over 250,000 registered organisations. There is no doubt in our minds that the continued growth of ISO 9000 is due wholly to marketplace coercion — larger organisations, in particular government organisations, obliging their suppliers to register to ISO 9000.

Even the most positive supporters of the Standard recognise it has limitations. Heralded as exemplifying "continuous improvement", the "year 2000" review represents a thorough re-write of the Standard. We would argue that this exercise is an admission of failure — failure of the Standard to make a positive contribution to economic performance. Of course, the institutions that have been built around the Standard must be expected to claim this to be an "improvement" — to do otherwise would undermine their credibility.

The new Standard (ISO 9000: 2000) is a substantially different document. However, much of the traditional ISO philosophy remains. The publication of a new Standard has occasioned the rewrite of this book. Five years on little of substance has changed, but re-reading our original work we have decided to strengthen some arguments and clarify others. For those unfamiliar with the Standard we have added a new chapter (Chapter 1) giving a brief history of ISO 9000. Chapters 8 and 9 are also completely new material. Chapter 8 is a critique of the process by which ISO 9000 has been reviewed and Chapter 9 is a critique of the revised Standard: ISO 9000: 2000.

We have little doubt that ISO 9000 will continue for the time being. The inertia caused by the institutions that surround it, and the marketplace coercion that gives it life, are unlikely to change in the short term. Because of this, and because the year 2000 Standard review has important weaknesses, we decided to publish a better alternative — the Vanguard Standards.

The Vanguard Standards[1] are a system thinkers approach to interpretation and use of ISO 9000. Systems thinking is, simply put, a better way to make the work work. These are, in our view, what ISO 9000 could have become if the authors had taken what we call a systems perspective — systems thinking being at the heart of quality.

An overview of the book

Chapter 1, A Brief History of ISO 9000, shows how ISO 9000 was adopted as a response to real problems, yet it was not the best solution. Understanding is central to improvement. Instead, ISO 9000 promotes a control philosophy. ISO 9000's plausibility, and the institutions surrounding it have led to growth in registrations world-wide, despite the lack of evidence of its benefits.

Chapter 2 offers a review of the available research. It is perhaps surprising that such substantial growth in registrations has taken place without solid evidence of the benefits. Research into the impact of ISO 9000 on organisation performance did not begin until many years after its promulgation. The research results should cause even the most optimistic supporter of ISO 9000 to have doubts.

Combining quantitative research, case studies and experiences in a variety of organisations, Chapter 3 lists ten specific arguments against ISO 9000. Chapter 4 then looks at what the defenders of the Standard have to say about our criticisms. In out view, nothing in their arguments represents a substantial defence.

---

[1] The Vanguard Standards are available to download (free of charge) from our web site: www.lean-service.com

Chapter 5 looks at the organisation as a system. The heart of our argument against ISO 9000 is that it has nothing to do with quality. Quality theory begins with understanding the organisation as a system. This theory is compared and contrasted with traditional "command and control" thinking. To illustrate the difference between a systems approach and ISO 9000, the application of a systems solutions to software quality (Tickit) is given.

Prepared with a systems view of organisations, the reader is taken through case studies in Chapter 6 showing what organisations did when registering to ISO 9000 and what they might have done instead if they had taken a systems view.

The argument that a systems perspective is the better way to understand and improve organisation performance is broadened in Chapter 7. The clauses of ISO 9000, by contrast, predictably cause organisations to do things that hinder performance.

Chapter 8 looks at the ISO 9000 review process. The fact of the review is an acceptance that ISO 9000 needs improving — but the process of the review led inevitably to confusion, something "quality" people should have been cognisant of.

Chapter 9 offers a critique of ISO 9000: 2000. The new Standard, while being significantly different, still maintains too much traditional (control) thinking and insufficient systems (improvement) thinking. The differences are discussed by reference to ISO 9000's eight quality management principles.

Finally, as an appendix we've included Japanese quality expert Takaji Nishizawa's Nine Principles for ISO 9000 Implementation.

Acknowledgements

This book has been written in collaboration with Richard Davis, Ibrar Hussain, Matt Loughran and Barry Wrighton. We are a group within the Vanguard consulting organisation who share deep concerns about what we have seen happening in organisations as a consequence of ISO 9000.

The Vanguard Standards were developed in conjunction with clients who wanted to use a systems thinking approach to the design and management of their organisation but who needed — because of coercion — to be registered to ISO 9000. We are grateful to those clients who collaborated in this work.

In the first edition of this book we acknowledged the influence of the work of W. Edwards Deming. It was Deming's work which first showed us the importance of understanding the organisation as a system. While we would re-assert our debt to Deming, we would also want to acknowledge Taiichi Ohno, the creator of the Toyota Production System, from whom we have learned much about the management of flow — central to performance improvement. His ideas have been used to strengthen some of the arguments in this second edition.

We are very grateful to Norman Burgess, Fellow and a past president of the Institute for Quality Assurance (IQA), for his help with ISO 9000's history. Takaji Nishizawa, a leading industrial consultant in Japan, came to the UK in April 2000 to conduct further case studies with us and we are in debt to him for the things we learned which are reported in this book. Last, but by no means least, Dennis Darker, a lead assessor and fellow of the IQA gave his expertise and time to a review of the Vanguard Standards.

Quotations from the Draft International Standard and Quality Management Principles[2] are reproduced with the permission of the International Organisation for Standardisation, ISO. Copyright remains with ISO.

John Seddon
August 2000

---

[2] ISO/TC176/SC2/WG15/N130/1997

PREFACE TO FIRST EDITION

It has been generally assumed that ISO 9000 registration makes a positive contribution to quality and competitive performance. The purpose of this book is to offer a different view. We shall set out the evidence and argue the case against ISO 9000 as a contribution to quality, productivity and competitive position. In simple terms, we shall argue that ISO 9000 makes you worse off, not better off. Our hope is that in taking an antagonistic position, we will provide a spur to managers who have little or insufficient knowledge of quality or who perhaps have developed indifference. Too many managers express the cynical view that quality is only concerned with "plaques and flags", an understandable view given what they have experienced.

ISO 9000 is a quality management standard supposedly aimed at improving economic performance. Our whole system is driven towards the adoption of ISO 9000. Government organisations and many of the larger private sector organisations insist that their suppliers register as a prerequisite for tendering. In the UK, Training and Enterprise Councils (TECs) have been measured on their ability to persuade organisations to register to it, and the Standard itself encourages organisations to impose a requirement on their suppliers to register. Today there are more than 52,000 UK businesses registered to ISO 9000, and about the same number of businesses registered throughout the rest of the world.

Since 1979 the British Government has taken an active role in ISO 9000's promulgation and today ISO 9000 has its own institutions: there are committees responsible for re-writing it and a multi-layered bureaucracy which licenses service organisations to live off the proceeds of assessing organisations against it. There are a plethora of training courses and armies of advisers and consultants, many of whom, armed with less than a week's training, sally forth as "experts" and impose their understanding of the Standard on unsuspecting managers who, on the one hand, feel obliged to follow suit and, on the other, hope only to improve their organisations.

Quality first came to the notice of business managers more than 50 years ago. It is still the most important and least understood subject on the management curriculum. Innovation and competitive position rely on being better, smarter and cheaper; quality thinking provides a method. Improving quality always results in greater productivity; improved productivity leads to lower prices and greater market-share. Quality provides the means to greater prosperity and a more secure future for organisations and their employees. But does ISO 9000 make a contribution in this regard? Our answer is an unequivocal *no*. This book has been written to put a spoke in the wheel of a phenomenon we have come to regard as seriously dysfunctional.

If the Standard and its institutions exist to make a positive contribution, it follows that a critical examination of their achievement can, ultimately, only improve what we are setting out to do. To develop our arguments against ISO 9000, we shall explore the Standard, what people do with it and what they might have done if they had taken a different view of the circumstances they faced.

By being labelled a quality Standard, ISO 9000 has only succeeded in steering quality into troubled waters. Far from being a first step to quality, it has been a step in the wrong direction. The hope is that it hasn't conditioned management to lose interest in the subject. If it has, it is only a matter of time before an economic jolt will wake them up. We don't want to wait until it's too late. We think the best way to regain management's attention is to be honest about the failure of ISO 9000. After all, there is a better way.

John Seddon
April 1997

In memorium

Matt Loughran

Chapter 1

A BRIEF HISTORY OF ISO 9000

During World War 2 the UK's Ministry of Defence had a problem — bombs were going off in the factories. To solve the problem they based inspectors in factories that supplied munitions. If you wanted to be a supplier, you had to write down the procedures for making your product, you had to ensure that your workers worked to these procedures by inspecting their work and finally you had to have this whole method of working inspected by a Government inspector. From this seed, a whole forest of control and inspection has grown in the name of quality.

This was a way of working which ensured that production met specifications. It was a method of control that was designed to ensure consistency of output. The inherent logic was quite straightforward and remains appealing — you control how you do the work and hence you make what you say you are going to make. These ideas solved a problem of the time — bombs stopped going off in factories.[1] Whether they went off when they should, whether they were better quality bombs, was another matter. "Quality" became associated with "conformance" rather than " improvement" and "quality assurance" implied that "conformance had been assured" through inspection.

---

[1] During one of many discussions of our views on ISO 9000, we met a man who had actually worked in a munitions factory during the War. He agreed that procedural control had solved the presenting problem. However, he informed us that other features of the factories were equally hazardous, yet they were not controlled because they were beyond the scope of the requirements! It illustrates a general problem with the control philosophy people only pay attention to that which is controlled.

The development of quality standards reflected the desire to shift the burden of work from inspection by Government inspectors (second-party inspection) to "quality assurance" guaranteed by the supplier through third-party inspection. In 1959 the United States developed Mil-Q-9858a ("Quality Program Requirements"), their first quality standard for military procurement. It laid down what suppliers had to do to achieve conformance. By 1962 the NASA space programme had also developed its "quality system requirements" for suppliers.

All of this effort reflected a genuine and serious concern. Many of our new technologies were causing us unfortunate problems. In 1962, Vice Admiral Rickover of the US Navy summarised the situation.[2] He spoke openly about what was happening in the nuclear industry. Things were going wrong; there had been a series of problems and as the US Naval Reactors Program grew in scope, things were getting worse rather than better. To quote his opening remarks:

> "Progress — like freedom — is desired by nearly all men, but not all understand that both come at a cost. Whenever society advances...there is a rise in the requirements man must meet to function successfully."

In short, he was concerned that the new nuclear technology was insufficiently understood and thus there were associated risks. To quote two later passages of his speech:

> "Unfortunately decisions affecting this field are sometimes made by people who have little knowledge of nuclear engineering and of science. There is a danger this will lead to errors highly damaging to the position of the United States or to the health and safety of the American people.
>
> Too often management is satisfied to sit in plush offices, far removed physically and mentally from the design and manufacturing areas, relying on paper reports for information about the status of design and production in the plant itself — the real centre of the enterprise. This lack of firsthand

---

[2] "The Never-Ending Challenge", a speech to the 44th annual national metal congress.

evaluation results in poorly designed and manufactured equipment, late delivery, or both. During the past few years, hundreds of major conventional components, such as pressure vessels and steam generators, have been procured for naval nuclear propulsion plants. Less than ten percent have been delivered on time. Thirty percent were delivered six months to a year or more later than promised. Even so, reinspection of these components after delivery showed that over fifty percent of them had to be further re-worked in order to meet contractual specification requirements."

These problems were not unique to the US military. In the UK, during the 1950s and 1960s, we were experiencing similar problems in all of the new industries. For example, in the power industry we had failures of turbine blades and boilers. Our nuclear industry was experiencing similar problems to those in America. These were problems associated with progress. Something had to be done and quality assurance seemed, to many, to be the answer. In 1968 NATO adopted the AQAP (Allied Quality Assurance Procedures) specifications — standards for the procurement of NATO equipment. The UK Government was, naturally, a signatory.

By this time, the idea of quality assurance had spread beyond the military. In 1969 the UK's Central Electricity Generating Board and Ontario Hydro in Canada developed quality assurance standards for suppliers. Earlier, in 1966, the UK Government led the first national campaign for quality and reliability with the slogan "quality is everybody's business". In the report of the year,[3] the following observations were made:

"The vital role of large purchasers — and the beneficial 'ripple effect' they can stimulate among their suppliers; their influences, through vendor rating and supplier quality assurance schemes, can help greatly to raise the level of quality procedures throughout industry. Consideration, however, could well be given to a more co-ordinated sys-

---

[3] Report on Quality and Reliability Year, British Productivity Council, in association with the National Council for Quality and Reliability, 1967.

tem of vendor rating to avoid the multiplicity of assessments
made by each customer."

At this time, suppliers were being assessed by any and all of
their customers. It was widely recognised that this was very
wasteful, duplicating effort and consuming resources unnecessarily. In 1969 Colonel G. W. Raby chaired a committee whose
task was to report on inspection and assessment of the UK's
military quality systems. His committee report reinforced the
idea that suppliers should take responsibility for quality assurance and recommended that their methods should be assessed
against generic standards of quality assurance. This was to
open the door to third-party inspection; it would lead to the es-
tablishment of assessing organisations. It would also lead to the
wholesale redundancy of many Government (second-party) assessors during the early 1970s. These people were to populate
the new assessing and consulting organisations, which were to
grow rapidly.

These first standards for quality assurance were thought of
as contractually binding obligations. During the 1970s the debate moved to how best to inspect and assure. Some commentators favoured a national body that would have responsibility
for assessment of suppliers; industry was not so keen on the
idea.[4] Meanwhile, in 1971 the British Standards Institute (BSI)
published the first UK standard for quality assurance — BS 9000,
which was developed for the electronics industry in response to
the many problems that were occurring in this, another new,
industry. In 1974 BSI published BS 5179, "Guidelines for Quality
Assurance"; the BSI was the natural home for the quality assurance debate and its leaders at the time were fully involved in
the developing assurance industry.

---

[4] British management has been characterised by Geert Hofstede (*Culture's
Consequences: International Differences in Work-Related Values*, Sage, 1980)
as having a "village market mentality", preferring serendipity and opportunity as the guiding traditions, choosing order only when it has clear
benefits. Hence British management's rejection of the European directives
on worker participation during the early 1980s and, more recently, their
antipathy towards what they see as the strictures of the Social Chapter.
There is little doubt that with respect to ISO 9000, British managers had no
choice: they were coerced into registration.

The UK Government was also very involved. Beyond the sponsorship of the "Quality and Reliability Year" in 1966, Government had management responsibility for many of the new industries. Half the UK workforce was employed in Government-owned or Government-subsidised industry. Power generation and distribution, extraction of natural resources, telecommunications and even automotive manufacturing were in Government's hands. It was in the Government's interest to do something to improve things. The Government also employed some 17,000 inspectors. The solution, when it came, must have appeared very attractive — at the same time as releasing thousands of people, Government could claim to be promoting the improvement of British industry.

During the 1970s BSI orchestrated meetings of the many interested parties in order to agree a common British standard. The result was the publication of BS 5750 in 1979. Key industry bodies that had developed contractual documents for suppliers agreed to drop their own standards and reference BS 5750 instead. In keeping with the historical perspective, the purpose of BS 5750 was to provide a common contractual document, demonstrating that production was controlled. This standard had nothing to do with methods for performance improvement. This shift in emphasis and the problems it spawned were to come later.

What were the key elements of BS 5750?

They can be summarised as follows:

- **Management responsibility:** Management should define and document a quality policy, an organisation structure, including responsibility and authority. Management should make available verification resources (inspectors), appoint a management representative and carry out management reviews.

- **Quality system:** The quality system must be documented, including a manual, procedures and work instructions.

- **Contract review:** A procedure for performing contract review — documenting what was agreed with the customer —

should be written, clearly stating the criteria for contractual obligations to be met.

- **Design control:** Procedures should define how the organisation designs its product and controls any design changes.

- **Document control:** Procedures and work instructions must be approved before issue and on subsequent changes. Control of documents should encompass availability, distribution, issue level, revision and obsolescence.

- **Purchasing:** Suppliers should be assessed and monitored, incoming goods should be verified.

- **Customer-supplied stock:** Customer-supplied stock should be subject to procedures for identification, inspection, storage and periodic maintenance. There should also be a procedure for reporting and recording lost or damaged stock.

- **Product identification and traceability:** A company-wide procedure should detail how items and equipment are to be identified at all stages from receipt to despatch. Where traceability is required, a unique identification should be used and recorded.

- **Process control:** Work instructions defining what is done should be documented and made available.

- **Inspection and test:** Inspection should be performed on receipt of goods. Documented procedures should define the appropriate tests. Tests should be performed for repair or service to demonstrate restoration of operative condition. Records should provide evidence to demonstrate the equipment or device meets the necessary inspection or test criteria.

- **Inspection, measuring and test equipment:** These must be controlled, calibrated and maintained.

- **Inspection and test status:** This must be identified by using markings, stamps, labels, routing documents, inspection/test record sheets, physical location or other suitable means.

- **Control of non-conforming product:** Procedures must define the controls used to prevent the use of non-conforming product. Items should be identified, segregated and the authority for disposition made clear.

- **Corrective action:** A corrective action procedure must be documented, defining what is to be analysed, how corrective actions are to be initiated and obtained to prevent re-occurrence. Corrective action procedures should be documented for dealing with customer complaints.

- **Handling, storage, packaging and delivery:** There must be procedures for all of these. Additionally, inventory must be controlled and procedures for warranty must be written and communicated to customers.

- **Quality records:** Procedures for identification, collection, indexing, filing, storage and maintenance must be written and records must be kept.

- **Internal quality audits:** These must be planned and scheduled to verify the effectiveness of the quality system. Audits must be performed by staff independent of the authority responsible for the area being audited. The procedures for audits, follow-up actions and reporting must be documented.

- **Training:** Procedures should be established to identify training needs. Training must be conducted on a formal basis and records kept.

- **Servicing:** If there is a requirement to service equipment, the servicing procedures should be documented and maintained.

- **Statistical techniques:** Statistical techniques should be used where appropriate.

BS 5750 was, in its essential content, no different from the methods used to stop bombs going off in factories. It was a method for the control of output. In response to the obvious problems we were having with our new technologies, this way of working was assumed to be a solution. At the end of the

1970s the standards movement had gained momentum. But its underlying theory was not good theory. While Vice Admiral Rickover — and many commentators since — lamented the state of management, this solution was to promote a theory of control, not a better theory of management. Perhaps we now have the benefit of hindsight, but would it not have been better to promote understanding rather than control? Admiral Rickover, discussing nuclear technology, saw management *understanding* as the priority:

> "More effective management and engineering attention should be given to the routine and conventional aspects of our technology. Nothing must ever be taken for granted. Management must get into the details of problems . . . analyse the cause of trouble by personal investigation, and take prompt action to prevent recurrence... Management and engineers must not conclude their job is over once drawings have been completed and the first component successfully built and tested to these drawings."

It is ironic that ISO 9000, what we would describe as the "control solution" to our problems, separated "design" from "process" (see page 123), making the understanding of this important issue less likely. It also served to maintain the tradition that management could and should be separated from work (see page 56), something Admiral Rickover, rightly in our view, saw as the nub of the problem.

He went on:

> "It should be of concern to us that specifications are normally written by manufacturers and therefore usually represent the lowest standard of engineering to which all manufacturers are willing to agree. This should be changed."

However, ISO 9000 ensured that it was not. ISO 9000 ensured that the manufacturer could determine its own quality system, provided it also satisfied the requirements of an inspector.

And he concluded:

> "Quality control must be recognised as an essential tool to enable management to meet today's technological imperatives."

But he did not say by what method. Admiral Rickover's address was probably the most open account of our failures with new technologies. The undisputed truth and alarming nature of the problems he described fuelled the urgency to "do something".

The same sense of urgency was being felt in British Government. In 1982 the Department of Trade and Industry published a white paper entitled "Standards, Quality and International Competitiveness".[5] It was to give a strong fillip to the emerging standards industry. Not only did it repeat many of the assertions of the leaders of the standards movement, it gave power to the BSI through a memorandum of agreement. The BSI now had Government backing to promulgate the adoption of the quality standard as quickly as possible and was authorised to represent the UK's approach on the world stage. The white paper also set out the arrangements for "certification schemes" and hence created the inspection industry we know today.

Again, with hindsight, one is bound to wonder what influenced ministers and officials. Clearly, the idea of international standards as means of entry to world markets appealed, but one wonders whether this was important for defensive reasons. The cynic might say it was important for control of those markets, and the evidence would bear him out. No doubt Government ministers were aware of the "Japanese miracle" (see below) and it is conceivable that they believed this quality management standard would deliver the same.

The British Government sought to "enhance the status of standards as an instrument of improving efficiency and the international competitiveness of British firms" by ensuring four things:

1. Closer co-operation between the Government and BSI to develop British Standards which are of the required quality,

---

[5] HMSO July 1982.

command respect in world markets and are suitable for regulatory purposes and/or for public purchasing;

2. Commitment from the Government to make greater use of standards where appropriate in its regulatory functions and to explore new ways of recognising standards;

3. A much greater emphasis in public purchasing on linking requirements to existing standards rather than technical specifications particular to the purchasers; and

4. The encouragement of certification schemes.

In doing this, the British Government set up the market and primed the pump. This white paper also began the confusion of "quality assurance" with "quality improvement". During the 1970s UK industrialists had visited Japan to learn about the "Japanese miracle". While they began to copy some Japanese practices, for example quality circles and suggestion schemes, they failed to "see" what was behind these practices — a fundamentally different way of thinking about the design and management of work.[6] Ignorant of this distinction, UK Government promulgated BS 5750 as a method for improving quality and economic performance. The Department of Trade and Industry funded "road shows" on the benefits of BS 5750 registration and provided funding to encourage organisations to use consultants in its implementation.

The recommended method of implementation was (and is) as follows:

1. **Look at your current organisation to see how it compares with the requirements of the Standard.** The Standard would ask you to consider such things as whether you had a formal way to review your contracts with your customers; whether your methods of working were documented and whether your manuals and procedures were kept up-to-date.

---

[6] The "Japanese miracle" was based on systems thinking rather than command and control thinking. We return to this distinction in Chapter 5. The Vanguard Standards (published at www.lean-service.com) are based on systems thinking.

2. **What corrective action is needed to conform to the Standard?** This is to ask "how should we close the gap?" What actions need to be taken to ensure we comply with the Standard?

3. **Prepare a programme of work**. It becomes important to establish by when all necessary actions can expect to be achieved. The focus of the work becomes achievement of the plan, in order to achieve registration.

4. **Define, document and implement new management system and procedures**. Documentation is always central to the plan, it is the means by which the inspectors can do *their* work.

5. **Prepare a quality manual**. This ties together all of the above. It is the starting place for inspection.

6. **Pre-assessment meeting**. The chosen inspector will often get involved in a pre-assessment meeting to help the client establish their suitability for going forward to assessment and thus registration. The interpretation of the Standard's requirements for the particular circumstances is the focus for discussion.

7. **Assessment**. The inspector determines whether the organisation conforms to its documentation. 'Do you do as you say you do?'

8. **Registration**.

Consultants and assessors provided much of the interpretation and guidance on the Standard's requirements. A correspondent whose career spanned the introduction of quality standards talked of his experience of the early period of BS 5750:

> "The greatest fear we all had was where the 'assessors' would come from. We knew in our hearts that it would be from the redundant Government inspectors and 'surplus' industry 'quality' managers. This has turned out to be the most disastrous part of the whole scheme. There are many ISO 9000 consultants I knew from their old industry days

that frankly I wouldn't have around, and now I find them
pontificating on how to run a business!"

The emergence of doubts about the value of the Standard and
the quality of advice on offer resulted in managers shopping
around for assessors, perhaps wanting to find the assessor that
would do the least damage; perhaps trying to find an assessor
who would add value. As long ago as the mid-1980s assessing
organisations were hearing their customers express serious
discontent with assessment and registration. These organisations responded by changing the role definition of their "visiting professionals" from "assessing" to "auditing". They argued
that the latter suggested they were in the business of providing
advice and guidance — it was driven by a recognition that they
needed to create value for their customers.

Yet this was to cross a boundary; an assessor should not be
an advisor, for that would open the possibility of undue influence. The original role, that of inspection, was the reason for
the Standard's origins. The assessor was just that, someone who
could relieve the customer of the need to check on suppliers (it
was assumed that checking could not be entrusted to the supplier). Now the role of the assessor began to be blurred: the
auditor became both poacher and gamekeeper. This of course
could lead to advice being tailored to meet the needs of the
paymaster. Does this shift of emphasis get us any closer to improving quality and competitive position, or does it run the risk
of taking us further away? There is, quite naturally (because the
system encourages it), evidence of abuse of the power of the
auditor's role. For example, one assessing organisation sets
targets for assessors to sell "value-added" services. Inevitably
this will lead to malpractice.

Extending the Standard's reach

Despite the growing discontent amongst organisations that
were using BS 5750, the BSI, with the backing of the UK Government, took the Standard to the international standards community. It was the British Government's intention to have British
standards earn respect in world markets. In 1987, BS 5750 became ISO 9000. It marked the end of a period of committee

work organised by the International Organisation for Standardisation and reflected a decision to promulgate the Standard throughout the international business community. The International Organisation for Standardisation (ISO), based in Geneva, is a worldwide federation of national standards bodies whose role is to promote the development of standardisation and related activities to facilitate the international exchange of goods and services. ISO 9000 was adopted to facilitate world trade. The basis for this decision is difficult to imagine, as there was a dearth of evidence available regarding the contribution made to economic performance.

For a document to become a standard it needs to go through committee drafts; then as a "Draft International Standard" it is made available to anyone who has an interest. A final draft is prepared following representations and it is put before the membership for formal voting. A 75 five per cent vote in favour is required for acceptance. In the first ballot of members, the Japanese would not support the adoption of ISO 9000 and the Germans only came around after much persuasion. However, the required 75 percent voting in favour was achieved. The die was cast. This standard — a standard concerning the way work is designed and managed — was now set to be promulgated around the world, despite the lack of evidence of its success and the obvious discontent amongst its users in the UK.

ISO 9000 — A way of managing for conformance

Quality assurance, according to the Standard, is a *way of managing* that prevents non-conformance and thus "assures quality". This is what makes ISO 9000 different from other standards: *It is a management standard, not a product standard.* It goes beyond product standardisation: it is standardising not *what* is made but *how* it is made. To use standards to dictate and control how organisations work was to extend the role of standards to new territory. To take such a step we might have firstly established that any such requirements worked — that they resulted in ways of working which improved performance.

Yet the plausibility of this Standard, and the fact that those who had an interest in maintaining it were (and still are) leading opinion, prevented such enquiries. In simple terms the Standard asks managers to say what they do, do what they say and prove it to a third party.

> ISO 9000 (1994) paragraph 1: "The requirements specified are aimed primarily at achieving customer satisfaction by preventing non-conformity at all stages from design through servicing."

To put it another way, the Standard asserts that preventing non-conformance achieves customer satisfaction. But does it? Of course it matters to customers that a product works. But there is no guarantee that the Standard will ensure even that. Furthermore, customers take a total view of an organisation — how easy it is to do business with — in respect of all things of importance to each and every customer.

ISO 9000 requires managers to "establish and maintain a documented quality system as a means of ensuring that product conforms to specified requirements". Loosely translated this is "say what you do". Management is supposed to "define and document its policy for quality . . . including its commitment to quality".

What management would not declare its commitment to quality? But would they know what it means? Would they argue (as they should) that quality management is a different and better way to do business, or would they believe that ISO 9000 will take care of quality? The Standard encourages managers to think of "quality" and "business as usual" as separate and distinct. It helps managers avoid the revelation that quality means a wholly different view of management. Instead, the organisation *"shall appoint a management representative who, irrespective of other responsibilities, shall have defined authority and responsibility"* [for ISO 9000]. At a practical level this means only one executive might decide he or she had better learn a thing or two about quality. However, would being responsible for ISO 9000 lead to learning about quality or simply enforcing the ISO 9000 regime in an organisation?

Key to the regime is auditing. The Standard requires organisations to conduct internal quality audits to *"verify whether quality activities comply with planned arrangements"*. This can be loosely translated as "do you do as you say?" and the purpose of the audit is to see that you do. It was not until the 1994 review that the words were changed to *"quality activities and related results"*. It was a Standard which was rooted in the philosophy of inspection: fifteen years after its initial promulgation the promoters sought to extend the focus to results. But results or improvements assessed by what means? Inspection. By the time the Standard was adopted worldwide, quality thinking had moved a long way from the philosophy of inspection. It is now understood, at least by a few, that quality is achieved through managing the organisation as a system and using measures which enable managers to improve flow and reduce variation (which we explore in Chapters 5 and 7). The defenders argue that there is nothing stopping a company having ISO 9000 and implementing methods for managing flow and reducing variation, but where are such companies? Few of the companies we researched, formally and informally, knew anything about this thinking. The Standard does not talk about it; moreover, the Standard effectively discourages managers from learning about it by representing quality in a different way.

According to ISO 8402 (quality vocabulary), quality is:

> "The totality of features and characteristics of a product or service that bear on its ability to satisfy stated or implied needs."

Everything we have learned about ISO 9000 suggests that the people who created this definition were thinking about the things which need to be controlled, those things which "bear on its ability . . .". The builders of the Standard assumed that customer needs would be listed in contractual agreements between the supplier and customer. ISO 9000 has a "make" logic — procedures for "how you do what you do" — and a "control" logic — check to see that it is done. It is a relic of the era when contractual agreements were perceived to be an important device for regulating the behaviour of suppliers. In these ways,

ISO 9000 encouraged "planning for quality".

Planning for quality sounds plausible, but it assumes many things: that the plan is the right plan, that it is feasible, that people will "do it", that performance will improve. It is an approach which, paradoxically, leads to poor decisions. Planners of quality systems, guided by ISO 9000, start with a view of how the world should be as framed by the Standard. Understanding how an organisation is working, rather than how someone thinks it should, is a far better place from which to start change of any kind.

Coercion resulted in growth

"You comply or we won't buy" has been the modus operandi for ISO 9000. In the UK, Government led the market by placing this obligation on all suppliers of Government, whether national or local. It resulted in some famous cases. For example Morris Men (country dancers) had to be registered in order to supply (dance for) a local authority. However, such humorous examples only provided respite from and ridicule of the more general sense of obligation and drudgery.

The growth of ISO 9000 registrations was monitored by the Mobil organisation until 1998, when this work was taken over by the International Standards Organisation. In 1998 the most recent of these surveys was published — there have been no published data since.

The number of registrations to ISO 9000 in the UK shows a slowing of growth as shown by Figure 1.1. The number of registrations in non-UK countries shows continued growth, as shown by Figure 1.2.

The number of countries using ISO 9000 has grown from 60 in 1994 to 143 in 1998. For the first time, the 1998 survey included information about ISO 9000 certificates being withdrawn. The main reason for withdrawal has been the organisations deciding to discontinue registration to ISO 9000. The leaders are the UK and Australia. In Australia almost ten per cent of registered companies have discontinued registration. To deregister is to swim against the tide of obligation. We know many senior players in the UK quality industry who want to de-register their companies but won't, for fear that it will be seen as not being concerned for quality.

Figure 1.1 ISO 9000 registrations in the UK

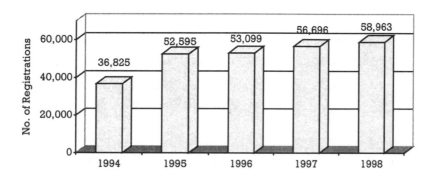

Figure 1.2 ISO 9000 registrations in non-UK countries

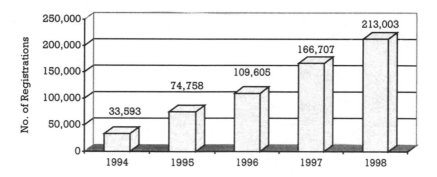

Where did we go wrong?

New technologies brought new and serious problems. Our response was to control rather than understand. The leaders of the control school led opinion and Government followed. Government set up the machinery for promulgation and marketplace coercion ensured growth. It is ironic that at the time our bomb factories were being controlled, some American bomb factories were being improved. This work was led by W. Edwards Deming, one of the figures who was to have a profound impact on Japanese manufacturing's quality and productivity. The methods employed integrated management with work, the essential solution sought by Admiral Rickover, and they were the secrets behind the "Japanese miracle".

The Japanese, Deming and others had a completely different conception of quality — it was concerned with methods for improvement, not control and conformance. We explore these methods and compare them with the methods promoted by ISO 9000 in Chapters 5 and 7. First we turn to the research on ISO 9000's contribution to economic performance.

Chapter 2

A REVIEW OF THE RESEARCH

By the early 1990s over 25,000 UK organisations had been assessed and registered to ISO 9000. The Director General of the British Standards Institute (BSI) asserted that these firms had improved the management of their organisations and enhanced their reputations for quality:

> "The benefits of applying BS 5750 are real; it will save you money — because your procedures will be more soundly based and more efficient; it will ensure satisfied customers — because you have built in quality at every stage; it will reduce waste and time-consuming re-working of designs and procedures. "[1]

However, we could find no evidence to support his claims. The growth of registrations to ISO 9000 had been paralleled by a growth in debate. Management magazines, national newspapers and quality conferences had all been involved in heated discussion between the advocates and critics. It seemed to us that such discussions were generating more heat than light. Our clients' persistent questions about the value of ISO 9000 registration led us to look for research which might illuminate what was going on and help them make informed decisions about whether ISO 9000 registration would be beneficial. We could

---

[1] *BS5750/ISO9000/EN29000: 1987, A Positive Contribution to Better Business: Executive guide to the use of national, international and European quality standards.* DTI publication.

find no research[2] that could help us understand what was happening, so we conducted our own.

In 1993 we published an extensive opinion survey, conducted in 647 ISO 9000 registered organisations. We now know the research suffered from problems of reliability and validity, as will become evident; but it was, nevertheless, useful in pointing us towards more fruitful lines of inquiry. The results raised interesting questions — people's perceptions may have been unreliable but the fact that these perceptions were held as opinions leads one to question why.

The 1993 research showed that only 15 per cent of the organisations surveyed believed they achieved all of the benefits claimed by the Director General of BSI; that is, improved efficiency, better procedures, less waste, lower costs and more satisfied customers. Some 69 per cent of the respondents believed that ISO 9000 improved "procedural efficiency", but the results for improvements in measurable aspects of efficiency (costs, waste, etc.) were only half as good, suggesting that the improvements attributed to new procedures were coloured by opinion rather than supported by evidence. One might expect people to believe that ISO 9000 had improved their procedures — implementation of procedures was, after all, the primary focus of registration.

These were not results which encouraged confidence about ISO 9000 registration, especially when one considers that the data were gathered from those who were likely to be well-disposed to it, the people who had championed ISO 9000 in their own organisations. The results raised questions as to whether the problems lay with the Standard, the implementers (consultants and managers) or both.

Other results from the survey can be summarised as follows:

---

[2] Up to this time (and since) the promotion of the standard as beneficial was politically rather than empirically-based. The various government-sponsored committees and institutions were populated by those who had an interest and belief in the "control philosophy".

- Most respondents (85 per cent) thought that, on the whole, ISO 9000 was a good thing, but that it suffered from problems of flexibility and interpretation.

- Government "organisations" were more inclined to insist on supplier registration to the Standard than private sector organisations.

- The Standard was implemented more from an "internal" perspective rather than driven by customer requirements.

- People reported that a "change in culture" was required to achieve success with ISO 9000 but there was a diversity of views as to what this meant.

- People's opinions differed in respect of whether the Standard encouraged the practice of listening to customers and whether it was important to introduce the concept of continuous improvement prior to implementation.

- People felt that the Standard had spawned many rogue consultants.

- People felt that management did not really understand ISO 9000.

- People who believed they succeeded with the Standard reported that they undertook it for broader purposes than those who undertook it mainly for reasons of obligation and opportunism.

- Smaller organisations had more concerns about costs and had greater expectations of improved market share as a result of registration. They also had more doubts about the Standard's relevance to their business.

It seemed that although the Standard was broadly felt to be a "good thing", there were many problems. Following the publication of this research, we visited five of the companies in the small group which had claimed ISO 9000 registration to be positive in all respects. In every case we found activity which was causing sub-optimisation, and which was present specifically because of registration to the Standard. It was a shock. It taught us not to rely on opinion data and it reminded us that managers — even quality managers — are often out of touch with what actually happens in their organisations.

We conducted a short telephone survey among the hierarchies of these five organisations: senior management were vague but positive about the Standard, middle management had issues with practicalities and workers saw it as another management initiative which caused more (and unnecessary) work. We still did not know enough about cause and effect — what were the likely consequences if an organisation went about registration to ISO 9000? By this time 14 years had passed since the Standard first appeared and we had no knowledge of its impact on organisation performance and competitive position. Consequently, we were unable to give our clients any more positive advice than we gave when they first enquired. We maintained our view that ISO 9000 registration was probably best avoided.

There had to be more to learn. Quality, we had come to understand, was a better way of doing business. Deming and others showed that as quality improved, productivity improved; it was a method of working which led organisations to greater economic security. But was ISO 9000 doing the same? Was ISO 9000 something which would benefit an organisation if approached in the right way? And if that was the case, why might some organisations succeed and others fail? Why didn't British management appear to understand it and was this important to the impact of ISO 9000 on performance? If senior management had understood it would they have been supportive or antagonistic?

Subsequent research conducted by Manchester Business School[3] and Surrey University,[4] both on behalf of assessing organisations, found similar results, although naturally these results were reported with a more positive "spin". The Manchester research, for example, was introduced by the sponsoring

[3] "ISO9000 — does it work? A report by Manchester Business School 1995"; commissioned by SGS Yarsley International.

[4] "Fitter Finance. The Effects of ISO9000 on Business Performance", commissioned by LRQA Ltd.

organisation with the claim that the answer to the research question — "does it work?" — was "a qualified yes". Yet no data were presented which could show why or how ISO 9000 works and plenty of data were reported which might lead one to have doubts.

The Manchester research included two findings which were heralded as proof at last that ISO 9000 was beneficial. The first was that *companies with ISO 9000 certification showed a significantly higher rate of sales growth than the national average*. The claim was based on a comparison of the sales growth of registered organisations with GDP, assuming GDP to be an indicator of "all organisations'" growth. Any competent researcher would observe that even if this finding were translatable into something meaningful, we would still know nothing about cause and effect. Another explanation for better sales growth in registered organisations could be that only registered organisations are able to tender for contracts; or possibly that all organisations in a sector are registered and the sector is growing.

The second "finding" was even more extraordinary. It was claimed that ISO 9000 registered organisations were *four times more likely to have survived the recent recession*. The foundation for this claim was an analysis of the progress of 185 companies which were first registered to ISO 9000 in 1991. Of the 185, 130 were still registered, 53 were still in business but no longer registered and 2 were no longer in business. These data were used to argue that the failure rate of ISO 9000 registered organisations was 1.1 per cent, which compared favourably with the national average for failures (5.2 per cent). One could equally have used this data to claim that *stopping registration to ISO 9000 won't harm your business*. It might have been more valuable to explore why the 53 decided they no longer needed to be registered to ISO 9000.

Anything more than a superficial reading of all the available research leads one to have doubts about what is going on. It is easy to see levels of dissatisfaction which are higher than ought to be tolerated, doubts about cost-effectiveness and concerns about assessors, waste (bureaucracy, paperwork, over-control) and the use of ISO 9000 as a promotional tool.

Despite the lack of evidence as to whether this way of managing is better than any other, those who gain financially from the Standard are, quite naturally, keen to promote its benefits. One of the assessing organisations ran a series of advertisements throughout 1996 claiming that ISO 9000 is *universally recognised, improves productivity, gives an organisation a competitive edge and pays for itself*. We (with others) complained to the Advertising Standards Authority (ASA) about the claim that ISO 9000 improves productivity. Our complaint was upheld. The ASA's ruling accepted the advertiser's view that ISO 9000 *could* improve productivity in some cases. But how could they know?

As opinion research had proved to be unreliable, we changed our focus to case studies. We were interested in finding out whether registration to ISO 9000 was predictably causing specific types of problems because of the Standard's implicit theory or the theories-in-use of assessors and consultants. We return to the case studies in Chapter 6.

A Visitor from Japan

As ISO 9000 has extended its reach throughout the world, we have received correspondence from many countries, becomimg a point of contact for all those who have doubts about the value of ISO 9000. Most correspondents have expressed their misgivings and catalogued examples of sub-optimisation. We introduce the following correspondent here because his work represents the latest piece of research. This was the first of a series of letters from Japan from a leading industrial consultant:

> Dear Mr Seddon, I read ISO 9000 News in July/August 1998 and learned about your book. I went to a bookstore and ordered your book. Now I am reading your book and I am in accord with your way of management thinking.
>
> I have been an industrial consultant for about thirty years. During this time I have done much improvement work (Kaizen) at client's factories and have written many books.
>
> Then ISO 9000 came. As in the UK, redundant government officers and surplus industry quality managers became assessors and consultants for ISO 9000 registration. Generally

they have not been familiar with JIT, VE, Taguchi methods and so on, which are concerned with true quality theory as you mention. Thus the similar problems you talk about in your book have occurred in Japan.

So I had to participate in the ISO 9000 movement to prevent installation of bad systems for my clients. In 1996, I was certified as a lead auditor and since then I have written several books and many articles on ISO 9000 introduction.

But generally, Japanese organisations are losing their world class systems by introducing the ISO 9000 management system.

Sincerely yours, Takaji Nishizawa

Takaji Nishizawa visited the UK in April 2000. The purpose of his visit was to study what UK companies were doing with ISO 9000. He told us that the Japanese had assumed they were unusual in experiencing problems with ISO 9000 and they were surprised to learn that the UK had problems too.

During his week in the UK, Takaji Nishizawa visited six organisations, accompanied by an interpreter and a Vanguard consultant. For us it was a return to the experience we had conducting case studies for the first edition on this book. Little had changed but Mr Nishizawa provided some important insights.

The results of this work are included at the end of Chapter 6, following the original case studies. To help the reader understand the perspective Mr Nishizawa took, we have to introduce some better quality theory (Chapter 5). Before that we need to make our case against ISO 9000.

The opinion research was, to say the least, cause for concern. Case studies and anecdotal evidence showed ISO 9000 to be having a negative impact on quality, productivity and competitive position. Putting all the evidence together, we have ten arguments against ISO 9000.

Chapter 3

TEN ARGUMENTS AGAINST ISO 9000

It was 1986. On a Friday morning in May a newly appointed director of customer services found a file labelled "escalation" in his in-tray. He asked his secretary what it was. "These," she said, "are the customers who may ring you next week with a complaint. It is the escalation procedure, it started when we did BS 5750. It ensures you know what is going on."

He soon found out that the procedure began during a Wednesday morning meeting with field engineers reporting to their managers which customers were unhappy. These managers brought their reports to superiors on Wednesday afternoons; the more senior group decided, during a meeting on Thursday mornings, which customers should go forward to the director's file. The director was furious. He issued an edict saying that in the future any customer who indicated unhappiness should be visited immediately by a manager who could understand the customer's problem and make a commitment to action. This, he insisted, should be the new procedure.

Next, the director called his assessor — the person from an organisation "accredited" with the competence to perform inspections. He was told that the assessor's job was to inspect the organisation as written in the physical documentation (manuals). If the procedures were judged as inappropriate by management, they should be changed and, if so, managers should remember to amend the documentation. (We visited this assessor seven years later. He had been closely involved with the early work on BS 5750 but now he was no longer an assessor. He told us that, in his

view, BS 5750/ISO 9000 had been the biggest confidence
trick ever perpetrated on British industry. It is easy to have
sympathy with his view.)

This "escalation procedure" was our first experience of BS 5750
(which became ISO 9000 in 1987). We had spent two years
studying the failure of quality programmes (usually training
courses, often labelled "Total Quality Management (TQM)", but
not treated as related to the Standard) and had become fasci-
nated by the teachings of the quality theorists. From what we
had learned about quality, the Standard did not appear to make
sense, and it bore no relation to what we had been learning.

We were persuaded to attribute the problem to inappropriate management thinking. The fault, it was argued, lay with
over-emphasis on bureaucracy and internal control. The argument was (and still is) "BS 5750/ISO 9000 is OK if you do it
right" (we return to this argument later). We now know that we
should have questioned this at the time, but the Standard was
new to us and it had the backing of government and institutions.
It was also hard to criticise something that was so difficult to understand. Furthermore, we were dissuaded from being critical,
as criticism was received as an indication that you were not a
supporter of the quality movement.

Through the 1980s and into the 1990s the bandwagon rolled
on. Marketplace obligation, even coercion, meant an ever-
increasing number of registrations. We witnessed a plethora of
companies registering and failing to achieve the promised result — improvements in customer satisfaction, efficiency and
other measures of performance.

The evidence suggests that registration to ISO 9000 leads to
sub-optimal performance. In simple terms, it makes performance worse. So many organisations have implemented ISO 9000
in such a way that it has added to costs, made customers unhappy, and demoralised staff; but most of all it has prevented
organisations taking opportunities to improve performance
which they might otherwise have seen. Registration to ISO 9000
has made "blind spots" of the means for improvement.

Our argument is that registration to the Standard has encouraged managers to act on their organisations in ways that

undermine performance. In all, a collection of influences —
current managerial thinking, consultants' advice and the
thinking implicit in the Standard, fuelled by the obligation to
register — have led to ubiquitous damage to economic and
competitive performance. It is possible, and we would argue
predictable, that ISO 9000 has inflicted damage to the competitive position of hundreds of thousands of organisations. It
is all the more disturbing that this should have occurred in the
name of quality.

Quality is defined in the mind of the customer, which leads
us to the first argument in the case against ISO 9000:

1. ISO 9000 encourages organisations to act in ways which make things worse for their customers.

> We called our telephone service provider with two simple
> requests. The service agent who took the call said she could
> action one of the requests but not the other, as it fell into a
> different category (one request was classified as a service
> call, the other as maintenance). This seemed silly to us:
> these were both quite straightforward matters which could
> easily have been noted for action by anyone. It was, we
> were told, because of ISO 9000. Clearly managers or advis-
> ers had interpreted the Standard in such a way as to make
> service more difficult for the customer. The organisation
> lost: we didn't take either service.

How often do organisations registered to ISO 9000 make customers run an "organisational maze" to get service (and pay
them for it)?

> Our printer announced that he could no longer supply us
> with quotations over the telephone. He had become regis-
> tered to ISO 9000 and this meant that paperwork had to go
> between us. Even using the fax we found that quotations
> now took at least four days.

The printer argued he was now a better quality company. We
(his customer) thought his quality was worse. We changed
printers.

One of the largest business-to-business printers in the UK was the first in its sector to register to ISO 9000. Five years on, because they were losing market share, they undertook an exercise in finding out what mattered to their customers. What they found surprised them. Customers wanted faster quotations and were buying from competitors because the competitors were able to give quotes in two days (compared to their average of ten). They reorganised the quotations department and processes. They got the quotations time down to a day and, the last we heard, they were aiming at getting it down to minutes by pricing and negotiating with customers over the telephone.

Stories like this lead the defenders to argue that the managers didn't have to do these things, they could have done the "right" things as part of their registration to ISO 9000. But the fact of the matter is they did not. What they did instead is something that is of vital interest. What happens in practice should help us to ask questions that would lead to a better understanding of the Standard and quality (and whether the two are the same). This behaviour was driven by the clause called "contract review" — the focus was on agreeing a contract, not understanding what mattered to customers.

Instead of doing what could have been done, these organisations, like many others, did things that made performance worse. It was of little value to the organisation above to have a well-documented and audited quotations procedure which was killing off their business. There are countless examples where an "internal focus" has led to worse performance, but in this case it was not just internally focused bureaucracy that was doing damage:

The quality co-ordinator had developed concerns about the Standard. In the drive for greater flexibility they had given more control of the work to the print workers and no longer wanted others (quality controllers) to audit their work. The quality manager had learned that checking increased errors. However, she was unable to convince her assessor that this was "good quality" (acceptable to his interpretation of the Standard). It resulted in record-keeping to serve the needs of the assessor and unnecessary "drudgery" as perceived by the print workers.

The bureaucracy impeded the relationship between the "value worker" — the printer — and the customer. The records, instead, became the way of managing work. Why? Because the Standard is concerned with control and inspection. The consequence is a loss of focus on what matters.

Records enable the inspector to do their job. The requirements for documentation are a major feature of the Standard: they represent the Standard's view of how one should go about checking whether organisations do as they say they do. The means for improvement lie elsewhere, but the documented system becomes the means for organisational control. Inspection means independent control of work, the "philosophy" of the Standard is grounded in "quality by inspection", but:

2. Quality by inspection is not quality.

Inspection increases errors, adds to costs and decreases morale.

> A Loss Adjuster was promoted to work in a larger branch. In her previous branch she had responsibility for her own work; in practical terms she signed everything she sent out. The branch manager in her new branch insisted that he signed all outgoing reports and typically he made changes according to his view of what constituted "good work". Within months the Loss Adjuster felt the quality of her work decline. She knew the branch manager would make changes according to his preferences and would, therefore, not take as much responsibility for ensuring the work was correctly completed. She knew the quality of her work was declining and she experienced a drop in morale, but she felt she could do nothing about it.

In such circumstances one often finds that the "inspecting" person does not inspect everything, assuming that the "worker" will have taken responsibility. Both parties are caught up in the psychology of inspection — each prone to assuming that the other will be responsible. It is a recipe for increasing errors.[1] Many people have doubts about the value of ISO 9000's requirements for external and internal inspections. Work records represent the most abundant and immediate manifestation of the Standard's ability to cripple performance.

> The joke in the transport cafés is that Eddie Stobart, a haulier whose quality of service has caught the imagination of British people, doesn't have ISO 9000. His truck drivers laugh while others talk about having to do their "second job" — having done the work, they have to write about it; they have to fill in forms for the records required by the quality procedures. When we learned of this, we called Eddie Stobart. He too was subjected to market-place coercion. People told him he might lose business if he did not register. But he had always felt that he ran a quality business and had good systems, and he distrusted the bandwagon which was surrounding ISO 9000, so he dug his heels in and did not register. He lost no business. There are others now who feel they might have been better off to have done the same.

In the late 1980s Tom Peters (business guru and best-selling author) observed that "quality in the UK has been taken over by the 'procedures merchants'". He struck a chord with many. Now ISO 9000 has spread to his home country (the US) as well as many others, despite the lack of evidence to suggest that it has a beneficial effect on quality and economic performance.

Working to procedures demoralises people. More than that, procedures are a terrible way to control work.

3. ISO 9000 starts from the flawed presumption that work is best controlled by specifying and controlling procedures.

This is why you find over-elaborate documentation, people having to do "two jobs" — do the work then "write" about it. You find documentation which only exists so that an inspector can do his job! These methods can result in activities that hinder

---

[1] And demoralisation — as became evident in the recent case of falsification of records at a UK nuclear installation.

people making a useful contribution, making them feel that the value of their contribution is, in whatever way, defined by procedures. Despite what many managers have been led to believe, to control performance by controlling people's activity is a poor way to manage. It is usually a fast way to sub-optimisation — it makes performance worse.

The following e-mail was sent to us by a government employee who was frustrated by the damage ISO 9000 had done to his organisation:

"Twelve months ago over 'two feet' of procedures arrived on my desk with the instructions that they were to be implemented immediately. Implementing those procedures increased our workload by, I would guess, 10 to 15 per cent. This was the start of ISO 9000.

We found that everything was detailed into sub-tasks for each procedure with a person responsible for each sub-task. But nobody was actually responsible for ensuring the overall activity was achieved. Innovation was totally stifled, the only way to do it was by the procedure. We had implemented some computerised bring-forward systems, more efficient but not in accordance with the procedures, so we had to go back to a manual paper system. Many procedures were written by people who didn't understand our jobs. In some cases the procedures were absurd in their impracticality.

Procedures were written on the basis of infinite time being available. Indeed threats have been made over the last year to work to procedure. There were so many of the damn things that nobody was ever sure if we were following all the correct procedures. If there was a task there was one or more procedures and signatures required at every point.

Twelve months later the amendments to the procedures are flying around at a furious rate to try and correct for the fact that people cannot (or, I have to admit in some cases, will not) follow all the procedures. The total cost of this exercise is circa £800,000 (excluding time spent learning procedures).

We got ISO 9000. Was it worth it? In my opinion, no. Talking to several major industrial companies, they will not implement ISO 9000 except where they are customer-facing and need it for PR purposes. Comments like "just a paper chase" are frequent. I work in a government department so the natural civil service way of working may have made things worse. The final straw today was a document which I am required to fill in yes/no. Unfortunately whoever revised the procedure had failed to actually add any questions.

Nice to see someone else admitting that the emperor has no clothes. Criticising 'quality' is like criticising the Queen Mum."

Consider what this correspondent said: "Nobody was responsible for ensuring the overall activity was achieved. Innovation was totally stifled." ISO 9000 did not encourage a focus on purpose. How many others experienced registration to ISO 9000 in this way? The question is important if we are to prevent others doing the same, but it is not a question which is encouraged. The government believes ISO 9000 to be "a good thing". If this e-mail is representative of what has occurred in every government department, the costs (borne ultimately by taxpayers) are fantastic. Obvious costs, such as fees to auditors and consultants, are significant, but the real costs are much larger — the costs of poor service, inefficiency and low morale become incalculable.

That organisations inflict such pain and suffering on themselves is itself an important phenomenon to understand. We believe it is inevitable when the principle reason for registration is coercion (see below). Managers are fearful about what could happen if they are not registered. The focus of management activity becomes "get it". It is vital to them to avoid the consequences they fear in not having it. Management, when focused in this way, does not learn.

To take one example:

Computer engineers working in Scotland had the reputation of being the best in their company. Every year the Scottish team won the service and quality awards. The company had decided it had to get ISO 9000 for its maintenance division (Government customers were demanding it). The first the

engineers knew about it was when a set of new work procedures arrived. On reading the procedures, the engineers
sent a message to the centre to say the procedures were
unworkable and, moreover, they would make performance
worse. The project team responsible for ISO 9000 implementation (in the centre) logged the engineers' message.
When we found it, four months had passed and no one had
been to listen to the engineers. The project team had been
targeted with getting ISO 9000 by a certain date. Managers
had decided what was important.

The managers and everybody involved with what they saw as a
"project" ignored its implications for performance. They did
not start with understanding performance, so how could they
have hoped to improve it? They started instead with the desire
to achieve registration to the Standard. Procedures dominated
over purpose. They were encouraged to work this way because
of the normal prescription for implementing ISO 9000, which is
our fourth argument in the case against ISO 9000:

4. The typical method of implementation is bound to cause sub-optimisation of performance.

It does not start with performance, it starts with a view of the organisation compared to a set of requirements. It is of course assumed that the requirements will, when properly interpreted,
have a beneficial impact on performance. But this is not proven,
nor is it theoretically sound.

The focus of implementation is to create documentation that
enables monitoring of the defined procedures. It is no surprise
that organisations get into the position where they ignore the
documented procedures until just prior to assessment — when
there is an unholy rush to ensure everything is in order for the
assessors. And the assessment is often a tortuous experience.
As we shall see, much of the assessor's training focuses on
"catching people doing things wrong". People do not like to be
"caught out" or controlled, they like to be in control. To be told
that a third party is the judge of one's performance is positively
de-motivational. When that third party cannot be bothered to
take an interest, it is even more destructive:

> Barry was working in an IT division of a large company. The division had decided to "go for" ISO 9000. So Barry's unit, like others, had documented what they did and had awaited the arrival of assessors. None visited his unit. There was a sense of being let down. The division succeeded with registration, but many like Barry wondered just what it had been all about and could not share the director's pleasure at the success.

Barry, like thousands of others who have been subjected to assessment, was ready to prove that he was doing what his procedures said he was doing. He was ready to show he was "doing things right", doing things according to the way they had been written down. But was he doing the right thing?

The better place to start change is to understand the "what and why of current performance as a system". When people (like Barry above) become engaged in these issues they become connected to the organisation's purpose and motivated to act. But this view of the world is not one that fits with the psychology of the "inspector".

5. The Standard relies too much on people's and, in particular, assessors' interpretation of quality.

Anyone can become an ISO 9000 consultant, but only those who have been trained (and passed) can become an assessor. A brief look at what such training comprises ought to be enough to make one worry about the power invested in such a group.

In summary, assessor training typically includes the following content:

- An overview of ISO 9000, its purpose and rationale

- Interpreting ISO 9000's clauses

- The role of the assessor

- Guidelines for auditing

- "Human" aspects: asking questions, dealing with conflict

- Writing reports

- Exercises and case studies.

No doubt there are assessors with extensive knowledge and experience (although we should always question the relevance of their experience to the needs of organisations today). Equally there are many assessors who know little, with only their newly gained qualification to guide them, finding themselves in positions of significant influence over the way our organisations work.

Contrast these circumstances with those of Toyota, an organisation that became the model of a "lean" system, producing extraordinary quality. The transformation of Toyota was led by experts — people who worked with a hands-on approach. Their learning was developed through action. The experts considered it normal to get "stuck in" in a practical way and make the necessary changes. By contrast ISO 9000 positions quality through the means of a prescription on how to ensure conformance — drawn up by our forebears — in the hands of (many) people who might have little or no hands-on experience. To make it worse, the auditor has power which, by and large, is exercised through observations of records and discussions in meeting rooms; talking about things, not doing things.

ISO 9000 involves an audit process where auditors compare what they observe against a set of criteria. The quality question might be: Has this audit process been tested? We have never seen a group of auditors being sent independently to an organisation with the purpose of assessing the reliability of their audits. The only available evidence we have, from trainees on assessor courses, would suggest that if we were to research this phenomenon, we would find inconsistencies between auditors.

> "Even the trainers couldn't always agree what the correct interpretation was. I was stunned at the implications — we (the trainees) could find ourselves out in organisations, wielding tremendous power and, at the end of the day, telling people to do things which *we* felt were important. All this power after only three days training!"

Another correspondent showed what the consequences of exercising this power were for him:

> "I was trained as a lead assessor. The emphasis was placed entirely on compliance with the Standard. Our quality manager thought this was wonderful stuff. We raised non-conformances by the truckload. Few were fixed at all, and those that were signed off were just cosmetic fixes. I don't particularly relish confrontation and certainly don't want to be associated with 'losing' situations. I'm afraid auditing can have a lot of both."

In our experience, assessors exhibit assumptions that influence the way ISO 9000 is implemented. In organisations registered to ISO 9000 it is easy to find examples of "just in case" thinking, people taking an unnecessarily pessimistic view of what could go wrong. This is to ignore the distinction between common cause and special cause variation (see Chapter 7) and leads to waste. Similarly it is easy to find examples of "keep people controlled" thinking, a legacy of the early days of inspection. The implicit belief is that people cannot be trusted. Yet organisations can only learn, improve and be motivational places to work when people are in control rather than controlled.

It is easy to find examples of "customers should all be treated the same" thinking. Yet customers want to be treated as idiosyncratic, individual, emotional human beings. All of these assumptions, which are all too common, make performance worse.

Assessors who hold these assumptions effectively have control over what is done in the organisations they are assessing, which leads us to the sixth argument in the case against ISO 9000:

6. When people are subjected to external controls, they will be inclined to pay attention only to those things which are affected by the controls.

Or, more simply: people do what you "count", not necessarily what counts. A correspondent illustrated the problem:

"The ISO inspectors are only shown certain areas for consideration — those that they know will pass. The company/site then uses the ISO 9000 pass throughout as a recommendation to customers. Manuals, whilst initially formatted, are not kept up to date. Records, generally, are not kept up to date. Records are often superficially modified just before the next visit. I could go on. There are many small problems — no one large flaunt.

These companies are very successful — they do not keep fully to ISO 9000, so why do we need it?"

In the case studies (Chapter 6) we describe Lan Co, a company that became so focussed on satisfying the assessor that they lost focus on their customers. The assessor wields significant power in the relationship; many managers feel they need to satisfy their assessor in order to keep their registration and thus be able to tender for business.

It is not people — workers or managers — that we should be controlling. Quality teaches us that continuous improvement relies on controlling work using different methods of control from those most managers are traditionally familiar with. At the time that our munitions factories were controlling output through ensuring that people worked to procedures, some American munitions factories were *improving* output by reducing variation. The work was led by Deming.

Following the war, Deming's ideas were ignored by American industry: a growing market tolerated the waste of inefficient production, organisations could pass their costs on to the customer. Indeed, Deming used to joke, "Let's make toast the American way: I'll burn, you scrape!" Approaching quality through inspection results in scraping toast. Inspection, Deming argued, was part of a wider philosophy that was flawed. He taught that a better philosophy was to understand and manage the organisation as a system, using the theory of variation to support decision-making. Our seventh argument in the case against ISO 9000 is:

7. ISO 9000 has discouraged managers from learning about the theory of a system and the theory of variation.

The theory embedded in ISO 9000's clauses does not encourage an understanding and use of systems thinking and variation in improving performance. Instead, ISO 9000 has encouraged managers to believe that adherence to procedures will reduce variation. In fact, adherence to procedures can increase variation — registration to ISO 9000 results in even more burnt toast! This is not to say that people should not "do things right". Clearly there may be advantages in some situations to working to standard procedures. But a different view would lead one to question whether we are "doing the right thing" and this is best determined by understanding and managing the organisation as a system and learning from variation. We know, for example, that in manufacturing, quality improves when variation is reduced. In service organisations, any variation from doing only what matters to customers will similarly drive up costs and drive away customers. Learning from variation requires measures, and measures, if chosen well and used in the right way, lead to learning and improvement.

Ignorant of the impact on variation, managers are easily persuaded of the benefits of having everybody working to procedures. It appears logical and commonsensical to think that people will do better if they are clear about what they have to do and work is orderly. But when is this true and when is it not true? ISO 9000 does not help us understand the answer because it assumes that it is always true. It starts from the presumption that it is of value to work to procedures; procedures which are documented, showing how work is done and inspected. ISO 9000 also provides the rules for inspection by others to make sure that "people are doing as they should".

Inspection translated into a contractual attitude between buyer and supplier: "You comply or we won't buy!" This is not an approach that fosters mutuality, trust and learning — the foundation for good customer–supplier relations. And this is our eighth argument in the case against ISO 9000:

8. ISO 9000 has failed to foster good customer–supplier relations.

The Japanese who followed the leaders of the quality movement learned to see their organisations as systems, systems which included suppliers and customers. From that point of view, entirely different (co-operative) thinking about how organisations, suppliers and customers should work together has developed.

ISO 9000, by contrast, encourages a "contractual" view of customer–supplier relations. Suppliers are obliged to show that they are registered. People in the customer organisations become focused on doing their job as designed by the Standard — "I am responsible for supplier assessment" — obliging suppliers to register or do other things which sub-optimise customer–supplier relations.

ISO 9000 reinforces an "arm's length" view of management, which in turn has maintained top management's ignorance about what ISO 9000 registration is doing to their operations in day-to-day practical terms. Without such first-hand knowledge, managers are unlikely to question either ISO 9000's or their own assumptions about how to manage. In so many organisations senior managers declare their policies as committed to quality, safety and the environment and then assume that ensuring all suppliers, dealers and agents are registered to the relevant standards will be a public example of this commitment. Unaware of the consequences they force others to comply and not complain; for to complain would be tantamount to saying you were not supportive.

Managers are not learning. The standards regime prevents learning.

9. Coercion does not foster learning.

If you wanted managers to be better managers, if you wanted managers to learn, would you put the choice of prescription for their learning in the hands of people who are not managers and then ask another group — who again are not managers — to inspect whether the managers are complying? Of course you would not. Yet that is what we have done with ISO 9000. To put it simply, a group of non-managers has dictated to managers what good management requires.

The locus of control is with the standard-setters and assessors, not with managers. Managers experience compliance rather than learning. Worse, for many this experience has turned them off quality for good for the experience has not been perceived by many to have added value to their business.

We see the same phenomenon in our schools today. We now have a regime of standardised curricula and inspection. If you talk to teachers following their inspection you find they experience a kind of emptiness. In much the same way as people in ISO 9000 registered organisations experienced the process, teachers spend many weeks and months preparing for the inspection, are anxious about its outcome and when the "all clear" is given, they experience a sense of loss, a sense of disappointment. It is quite simply because the locus of control is with the assessor — it is robbing people of pride. This consequential de-motivation — the most debilitating form of sub-optimisation — is, in large part, a natural response to being controlled. And ISO 9000 starts, *a priori*, from an attitude of controlling people, which leads to bizarre but understandable behaviour.

The drive to be able to tender for business is the reason for managers being prepared to pay for "ready-made" manuals and obtain fraudulent assessments. It is a natural response to coercion: people "cheat" — they do what they need to do to get by, to avoid the feared consequences of (in this case) not being registered. Managers are not learning, which leads us to the final argument in the case against ISO 9000.

10. As an intervention, ISO 9000 has not encouraged managers to think differently.

ISO 9000 has taught managers little or nothing about the most important subject on any management curriculum — quality — and it has probably made many of them averse. Some managers and certainly the majority of assessors believe an organisation has "done quality" having registered to ISO 9000, when nothing could be further from the truth.

ISO 9000 represents further reinforcement of the idea that work is divided into management and worker roles. It was *the* fundamental mistake of 20th century management, for the Standard continues the tradition that "managers decide" and "workers do". This tradition has led to means of control, through adherence to budgets, targets and standards. To this view of management "adherence to procedures" is attractive. However all of these things — management by budgets, targets, standards and procedures — all cause sub-optimisation. They are the causes of waste in our organisations. Worse, this way of thinking about the design and management of work inhibit innovation. To innovate, we need to thinking of our organisation from the customers' point of view; we need to manage processes end-to-end; we need measures related to purpose in the hands of those who do the work. These prerequisites for innovation are components of managing an organisation as a system, something at the heart of quality thinking. This way of thinking is diametrically opposed to prevailing thinking about the design and management of work, which can be summarised as "command and control" thinking. ISO 9000 was conceived in and reinforced a "command and control" mentality.

We shall explore the nature of "command and control" management thinking and question its relevance for the problems and opportunities our organisations face today. Changing our thinking about management is the key to performance improvement.

The better way starts with understanding the organisation as a system. It implies a completely different management philosophy. The Japanese companies that adopted this philosophy achieved remarkable results. In the UK we have worked with a variety of organisations that have achieved rapid improvements by adopting this different philosophy. We introduce the concepts of systems thinking in Chapter 5, but firstly, having presented our arguments against ISO 9000, we shall discuss what is said in defence of the Standard.

Chapter 4

IN DEFENCE OF THE STANDARD

Advertising had been telling managers that ISO 9000 registration was not only a "good thing", but also a necessity. Governmental and larger organisations had been obliging their suppliers to register. ISO 9000 was assumed to be good for business. When we published our 1993 research we questioned this assumption. Further, we argued that if, as a business community, we were committed to quality, then surely we would want to be satisfied that anything we were doing to improve it was tried and tested or "fit for purpose". To carry on with something that was clearly showing equivocal results would not be a "quality" response, but was tantamount to burying one's head in the sand while the economy was suffering.

Research and anecdotal data were suggesting that registration to ISO 9000 was a guarantee of sub-optimising performance. It seemed to us that this "emperor" had no clothes. We took this view to those who were promoting the Standard as a requirement for doing business. We held discussions on the internet, in the press and with managers and quality professionals in a variety of forums. When you publicly criticise something that is regarded as a requirement, you expect to be under attack from those who have a vested interest. We were. It is regarded by some as audacious and irresponsible to criticise ISO 9000. In a nutshell, we have argued that this Standard is bad for business. This has not gone down well with the Standard's defenders.

When confronted with the evidence of failure, the defenders employ the following arguments:

"It's OK if you do it right."

This is at least an implicit recognition of the fact that people are having problems. Is it a satisfactory defence? The argument goes that "proper implementation is vital" and "interpretation is not the fault of the Standard". It probably goes without saying that this is the favourite argument of those who make their living from ISO 9000. They would have us believe that there are good and bad ways of "doing ISO".

It is a terrible argument. How many good ways? How many bad? How will we know? Who can we trust to tell us? How many have suffered at the hands of bad advice or misguided interpretation and what has this already done to competitive performance? How is a manager to make a choice? How can it be a decision based on the confidence that one can predict an improvement in performance? Should managers just soldier on in the hope that they hit on the right answers or find the right advice? How many sources of advice should they tap before they are satisfied that the one they choose to follow is the right thing to do for their business?

"It's OK if you do it right" is not a sustainable defence. Furthermore, it ignores the evidence that shows how the Standard specifically encourages actions which cause sub-optimisation of performance.

The defenders of the Standard would have us believe that the Standard cannot be blamed, as though this was a reason to defend it's promulgation. An ISO 9000 consultant, defending the Standard in an Internet discussion, put it this way:

> "It is not the Standard ipso facto but its use which has so seriously gone wrong (bearing in mind that there are well known defects in the Standard which are at present being addressed). For this I have sympathy with the right-minded but poor consultancy-duped managers, but not too much for the cynical 'I'll have a bit of that' managers who don't want to know what that is or how they have to change their attitude to implement it properly."

Leaving aside the problems of "it's OK if you do it right" implicit in his first argument, he is right. He asserts that it has gone seriously wrong. Whether the defects are "well known" (especially by managers, the constituency which ought to know) and will be addressed, is open to question. He is right to say that managers' attitudes need to change if they are to understand quality. But managers have to be helped with an explanation of how their attitudes need to change and many who have experienced the excesses of the Standard will already have negative attitudes to what has been sold to them as "quality".

The same correspondent laid the blame on government ministers. But it does not help to lay the blame on government. If we did, government would be obliged to turn to the decision-makers of the quality movement. If they did, they would likely find equivocation, defensiveness and the assertions that "it will be all right eventually" or "change takes time". But the evidence suggests that registration to ISO 9000 makes performance worse. The defenders ignore the practical evidence. When presented with what has actually happened in practice they blame anything or anyone rather than accept that we have a problem. What is extraordinary is that people who work in organisations will readily acknowledge that there is a problem, but the "ISO 9000 industry" has a critical mass which makes it appear deaf and unstoppable. The mountain of institutions, experts, publications and organisation appointees which constitute this "industry" casts a very large shadow over the evidence of what is happening.

"ISO 9000 is a minimum standard or a 'first step' on the quality journey."

Taking the notion of the Standard being a minimum, one ISO 9000 consultant said:

> "I stress minimum because failure to recognise this important aspect leads to misplaced anger when results do not stack up to expectations."

It interested us that this correspondent implied that managers should be warned that they should not expect too much from ISO 9000. We would want managers to expect a lot from quality.

After all, it is a far better way to run a business. But is the Standard a "first step"?

The notion that ISO 9000 is a minimum standard implies that there is a continuum — it is often expressed thus: "quality starts with ISO 9000, and progresses through TQM to world class".

For there to be a continuum, one should be satisfied that points on the continuum reflect ever-greater emphases of the underlying principle or philosophy. That is, "world class" operations should show the same basic principles as ISO 9000 registered operations, only in greater degree. However, in every case we have studied, ISO 9000 registration has represented a step in the wrong direction. It has, for example, maintained the division of labour between doing work and decision-making. It has maintained measures that are associated with a traditional "command and control" view of the organisation. It has, effectively, cemented in such practices.

In world class operations, decision-making is in the hands of people who do the work and they use different measures from those we are used to in "command and control" organisations, and these alternative measures are essential prerequisites for flexibility and learning; they are concerned with understanding and improving flow. To understand how to make such changes, managers need to change their thinking about measurement. To do that, they have to change their thinking about how to design and manage work. Adopting the Standard in no way facilitates that change; it hinders it.

The distinction is philosophical. It is about the management, or more specifically the control, of organisations. The thinking about control implicit in ISO 9000 is diametrically opposed to the thinking about control in world class operations. What we have learned is that putting control of processes in the hands of people doing the work results in more learning, pride and, in fact, more and better control.

ISO 9000 is predicated on the plausible idea that procedures are the prerequisite for control. It is a notion that has "common sense" appeal. One correspondent expressed it this way:

> "We all work to procedures in some way, form or other in our daily lives. Voluntarily and involuntarily. Our own indi-

vidual life style in the modern world is built around procedures. Some written in law and others by habit or etiquette. Without the visible and invisible rules we would surely drop into chaos.

This analogy can be equally applied to the workplace in any environment. The company takes the view that it wishes to make money. In order to do that it must make or do something that attracts customers. To maintain customers and to broaden its sales area it must go on satisfying customers. To ensure that this philosophy is understood by all a policy is established which is supported by a set of rules that govern output. The management maintain control over its production or service. Discipline is maintained and output stabilised."

This is the "bomb factory" argument. Control of procedures will control output. But quality is concerned with improving output. Another correspondent understood this distinction:

"In its basic form it is a tool that can be used as the foundation of a control structure that regulates and introduces consistent operations within an organisation. An approved system can go a long way to giving assurance to a customer that there is some level of control on how operations are conducted. It does not, and never has, assured good quality output."

Should we be heartened that the output of our organisations is controlled or dismayed that we have stifled learning, innovation, flexibility, improvement and damaged our competitive position? When we embarked on this journey did we seek "control" or "improvement"? Perhaps this is at the heart of the problem: a standard which solved a control problem was subsequently labelled as a solution to quality problems. There is a discontinuity between the theory of control as expressed in ISO 9000 and the theory of control as expressed in world class operations.

There is a further argument used by those with a "procedural-control" view of the world. To quote an ISO 9000 assessor:

"Before a process can be improved, it must be established
as a set of procedures which people conform to."

This is both true and not true. It is true when the organisation is
focused on managing flow. In the Toyota Production System
procedures are totally standardised; but the workers are focused on achievement of purpose and have control over the
line. In "command and control" organisations, procedures are
set, *a priori*, from an internal and functional perspective. In such
circumstances the first thing that should be done if one seeks
improvement is to find out what is currently going on and why.
This starts with measurement — measures of what the process
(or processes) is predictably achieving and measures of what is
predictably going wrong. Only if a process is entirely unpredictable might it be necessary to establish and work to procedures in order to learn more about what is going on.

When you set about establishing how well processes
achieve their purpose in "command and control" organisations,
you often find that they are stable but exhibit wide variation.
The variation is, most often, caused by "tampering" — managers paying attention to output data (targets, standards, budgets), causing people to "do whatever it takes" to meet the required numbers. Measures of work are often distorted by managers bringing work backwards or forwards in order to "make
their numbers". Variation caused by such tampering only
makes it harder to learn about what is going on in the proc-
ess(es).

The argument for first establishing procedures reflects a
control view of the world. By contrast, to establish what is happening, and why, is to start from a position of wanting to learn.
To establish what is happening and why requires managers to
take different measures and use them differently, it requires
that they understand the theory of a system and how to learn
from variation (we return to this in Chapter 5).

Management behaviour is governed by management thinking. Which is why the next argument used by the defenders is
so disturbing:

"ISO 9000 is no more than basic good management practice."

The problem is it is a document crafted by people who think of management in a particular way. To argue that ISO 9000 is no more than a basic good management practice tool takes no account of the nature of what is written.

One defender who subscribed to this view described ISO 9000 in the following way:

> "1. It sets a basic level of customer assurance through certification.
>
> 2. It enables management to visibly apply the invisible rules they always had.
>
> 3. The exercise buys the workforce into the scheme; thus it becomes self-perpetuating.
>
> Lest we forget our focus."

Taking each of his arguments in turn: There is plenty of evidence to show that certification (we are using the term "registration") cannot be relied upon to assure much. It might be what was intended, but registration is no more than a form of control and, as such, can be relied upon to guarantee little or nothing. People are adept at getting around controls.

To assert that ISO 9000 enables management to "visibly apply the rules they always had" is precisely our point. ISO 9000 is no more than a particularly inefficient application of traditional management thinking — it sets out to control people's behaviour through procedures and inspection — the very thinking which needs to change if we are to establish quality as a way of life in our organisations.

To take his third point, although we hear a lot about "workforce participation" in ISO 9000 registration we have yet to meet a workforce which speaks well of working to the requirements of the Standard. On the contrary, ISO 9000 has been a major cause of demoralisation and it is easy to see why. In most cases the work procedures have been imposed on the workforce. It is argued that the enlightened way to go about registration is to have the workers involved in writing their own procedures. But in these cases too the consequence is often a lowering of morale. ISO 9000 imparts a philosophy of working to procedures rather than working to improve performance against purpose.

Finally, to argue as he does that ISO 9000 is of value in reminding people of the organisation's focus is to place value on the "contract" between them and their customer and the associated "procedures" for its delivery. This is not a quality focus, it is no more than focusing on "doing what we say we do". The value created by organisations for their customers goes beyond the performance against contract. The customers' view of any organisation is made up of the whole range of transactions they experience. The focus of an organisation wanting to improve quality and competitive position should be on learning, not compliance.

The idea that organisations should adhere to their contracts with customers is laudable and would be a significant benefit to our competitive position whether it were achieved through ISO 9000 registration or any other means. But ask any manager about their experiences of ISO 9000 registered companies and you will find plenty of evidence which casts doubts on the claim that ISO 9000 is a guarantee of an organisation's ability to meet its contractual obligations.

ISO 9000 is not "good management practice", it reinforces the idea that it is management's job to decide and the workers' job to do. As a management tool it is no more or less than "more of the same" — it is "command and control" by prescription.

"There is no choice, it is a requirement for doing business."

A real but sad reflection of what has occurred in the world marketplace. An American correspondent put it this way:

> "It's like a freight train coming down the tracks — you're either on it or on the tracks."

People now believe it is an absolute requirement for doing business, despite evidence to the contrary. The growth in registrations has been achieved through marketplace coercion, by instilling fear of what may happen if an organisation does not register. The only way to diminish coercion is to create a wave of opinion against it. The few that have not succumbed to coercion have not lost out. In fact, they have won. They are without the encumbrance of the Standard, they have not felt the need to argue as others have done:

"It is important for defensive reasons."

This argument goes that we need ISO 9000 for the same reason as we have other (product) standards — they can provide protection in the contractual sphere to the extent that, when a party claims to be operating to a standard, then they can be held to that standard if in breach (non-conformance). We are ill-served by a contractual and defensive view of customer–supplier relationships, and even though the Standard can be used as a card in disputes between customers and suppliers, few do so because the Standard does not and cannot guarantee the quality of the product, nor even that the product will be delivered on time. The real defence is avoiding being the odd one out. Everybody's doing it because everybody's doing it:

"It must be good, 200,000 companies can't be wrong."

We have over 58,000 registrations in the UK, the remainder are spread around the world. There are no data to show that it has any value in terms of organisation performance but it has been promulgated as worthy. Organisations are abiding by a requirement when there is no evidence that it is the right thing to do. In the American civil war field surgeons swore by their methods which, because of their ignorance of germs, were actually killing many of the wounded they treated. This is analogous to the situation we have with ISO 9000. It is making the patient's condition worse, but it reflects the views of those who control the quality movement — the "field surgeons". How many "patients" have to die before we take a look at what is going on?

The volume of registrations is a reflection of marketplace coercion. We are confident that without marketplace coercion, registrations to the Standard would not be growing, for it has little intrinsic value.

"It is being improved"

Even the defenders of ISO 9000 are open about what they see to be the Standard's limitations. They would not go so far as to stop it, perhaps not least because many of them are dependent on the Standard for their living. They argue that, with improvements, the Standard will serve its purpose. We discuss whether the latest "improvements" are in fact improvements in Chapter 9. But for now it is important to note that the implicit failure which this line of argument accepts is never quantified, measured or costed. It is one thing to declare that ISO 9000 needs improving, but how will we know it has improved if we have no measure of the extent of its current failure? Should we simply have faith?

We think not. It would be to have faith in the unproven. It would be to blindly follow when managers would be better to have their eyes and minds open. In our experience in order to improve performance, organisations registered to ISO 9000 have to unlearn and undo much of what they have implemented. They first need to learn how to understand their organisation as a system.

Chapter 5

THE ORGANISATION AS A SYSTEM

It was in the late 1940s and early 1950s that a group of Japanese manufacturers began to understand and manage their organisations as systems. They learned that it was unhelpful to think of organisations as functional hierarchies with budgetary controls. It was to think again about something which (in Western industrialised countries) had become "normal". The Japanese pioneers were aware of how traditional mass production methods resulted in sub-optimisation. This is not to say that mass production organisations did not (and do not) work; they were an innovation which resulted in economics of scale. They discovered that organisations could improve further but only by taking a different view, a systems view. A systems view provides the means to manage flow. The result, by comparison, is to achieve what might be called economics of flow — a quantum leap beyond economics of scale.

Taiichi Ohno developed these ideas to extraordinary benefit in the Toyota Production System. Shigeo Shingo did likewise in Matsushita. These ideas were the secrets behind the "Japanese miracle", they represent a different and better way of designing and managing work.[1] They are not found in ISO 9000's clauses.

Most of our organisations are designed and managed according to the principles of "command and control". This is not to do with being "bossy", it is a logic about how to design and manage work.

---

[1] For wider reading on the principles and practices of a systems view, visit www.lean-service.com

Figure 5.1 Command and Control versus Systems Thinking

	Command and Control Thinking	Systems Thinking
Perspective	Top-down hierarchy, functional procedures	Outside-in, process and "flow"
Attitude to Customers	Contractual	What matters?
Decision-making	Separated from work	Integrated with work
Measurement	Output, targets, standards: related to budget	Capability, variation: related to purpose
Attitude to Suppliers	Contractual	Co-operative
Ethos	Control	Learning

"Command and control" management thinking begins with the separation of "decision-making" from "doing" and hence it defines management's role (as decision-making). Work is typically designed in functional specialisms and "control" or decision-making is exercised through financial budgets or work targets and standards. The work of management becomes "paying attention to output": monitoring of numbers, standards or specifications, in the false but plausible assumption that improving the numbers is the same as improving performance. It is a way of managing which guarantees sub-optimisation. It causes waste, it prevents managers from understanding how and why their organisations perform as they do. Consequently, managers can often act in ways which makes things worse. Worst of all, it is a way of managing which damages morale.

We are confident that "command and control" management thinking will be abandoned.[2] Managing from a systems perspective is far more economically beneficial. If "command and control" is not abandoned, our organisations will remain sub-optimised and even more importantly, their "creative anarchy"

---

[2] The only hurdle in abandoning "command and control" is the preparedness to challenge current thinking — a significant hurdle.

will never be unleashed; we will not learn, innovate and change. Without optimisation, learning, innovation and change we will cease to compete effectively in the world economy.

> There is a story about a Japanese guru, working with the board of management of a British organisation. His job was to recommend how they could improve performance. He prepared a list of recommendations and the first recommendation was "the board should resign". He got the board's attention, but the point he wanted to make was "if you don't change your thinking, nothing will change".

Figure 5.2 Thinking Governs Performance

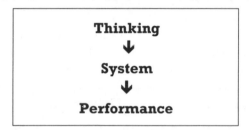

People's behaviour is governed by the system they work in. In turn, the system is governed by the prevailing management thinking. Interestingly, this helps us understand why so many programmes of change fail. When they fail it is generally because the attempt was non-systemic — there was no change to the system and, by implication, no change to management thinking.

Understanding why change programmes fail is one way to get to grips with systems thinking. Often, for example, they fail when people are trained and put back into a system which is not designed to "let them do it". To take a simple example: training everybody in customer care assumes that if people do "as they have been trained" with customers, customer service will improve. In practice, the behaviour of people who deal with customers is governed by their system. It is management who put in place the work functions, information, roles, procedures and measures which create the system which either helps or impedes service and learning (improvement). It is the system that is often, in fact, preventing change. It is not unusual to find that 90 per cent or more of variation in service performance is caused by the system. Managers are focused (wrongly) on the 10 per cent (or less). Consequently they waste resources on ineffective interventions.

For example, should a service engineer be in your home and unable to repair your appliance, his behaviour at that point will be determined by the system he works in. There are three things in a service engineer's system: call despatch, who tell him where to go; logistics, who provide him with parts, and his manager. If each of these parts of the system is designed to fulfil its own purpose, rather than the common purpose — if call-despatch people are measured on calls they take, their focus becomes "take calls", not help the engineers to route efficiently and meet commitments to customers; if logistics is measured on inventory costs, so they make it difficult for engineers to get spares and the decision to hold spares is always made on the basis of cost, not service to the customer; if managers are measuring engineers' activity, assuming that increasing activity increases productivity — the engineer will be unable to make and meet a commitment to you, the customer. In a badly designed system, no amount of customer-service training for engineers will make a difference.

In examples like this you always find waste: "failure" calls in to call-despatch; rework and "over-work" on customers' premises; lost and faulty parts in logistics and so on. These are caused by the system and that is the responsibility of management.

The failure of programmes of change is masked by both the plausible aspiration to "do things right" and the rationalisation that "change takes time". Unfortunately, there is not much questioning as to whether the programmes were the "right things to do". Many programmes of change, despite the fact that they appear to have the right labels ("customer care", "quality", "co-operation", "teamwork"), fall far short of success because there is no change to the system. In the case of ISO 9000, the focus of implementation is typically "what do we need to do to achieve registration?", regardless of whether these actions will facilitate or impede performance improvement. Here we discuss what it means to understand and act on an organisation as a system — and contrast this with traditional "command and control" management thinking — because it is from a systems perspective that we make our case against ISO 9000.

Flow, not function

A system is a whole made up of parts. Each part can affect the way other parts work and the way all parts work together will determine how well the system works. What matters is how work flows through the system and how the parts of the system affect that flow. Taking this view has profound implications for what it means to manage. Traditionally we have learned to manage an organisation by managing its separate (functional) pieces (sales, marketing, production, logistics, service, etc.). Managing in this way always causes sub-optimisation. Parts achieve their goals at the expense of the whole; people do what they have to do to "make their numbers" (for example, "sell what you can get away with"), even if this means a loss to the system (poor quality sales resulting in returns and/or customer dissatisfaction).

Outside-in, not top-down

A systems view of an organisation starts from the outside-in. How does this organisation look to its customers? How easy is it to do business with? The focus is: how well does the system respond to the demands made on it by its customers? To begin an analysis of an organisation as a system, the place to start is at the points of transaction with the customer.

For example, how does an intruder alarm company look from the outside-in? To keep it simple, we will start at the point when a salesman has been given an order. We must assume that the customer is happy, he or she has parted with half of the payment (common practice in selling intruder alarms). Next the customer sees an installation engineer. We want to know what happens predictably now. How often does the engineer arrive on time as committed to the customer? How often is the engineer able to complete his task without a hiccup? Here's what we found in one particular case:

> There were many customers complaining that they were waiting for installation. We found that when installing, the engineer had to ask customers about the siting of equipment — things the customer had covered with the salesman — and, furthermore, the engineer often found that he did not have sufficient equipment to complete the job.

What is predictable?

A systems view leads managers to ask: what is predictable about the process — what will happen in the future if nothing changes? Management by prediction is the hallmark of systems thinking. How predictably do these problems occur? In this case we found there were no jobs which went without a hiccup at installation. One hundred per cent failure, predictably, which means that if nothing is changed the same will happen in the future, next week and the week after. Imagine the costs — the costs of bad "word-of-mouth" from customers who are not happy waiting, the inefficiency associated with having to return for equipment, the impact on the customer of being asked the same thing twice. (Also note that few of these costs will be seen in traditional, functional measures.) Now we have to ask why this is happening. The fact that it is common and predictable is good news (however bad the impact) because if something is happening predictably, it is being caused by the system and that is under management's control. In this case it was easy to see why.

> Salespeople were targeted on revenue. Because they were focused on "making their numbers", rather than ensuring that the organisation delivered a quality service, they would do anything to get a sale; for example, leave cabling underestimated (to keep the price down) or specify insufficient parts. They would also tend to leave documentation in an unfinished state, causing administration to search for missing information before scheduling an engineer. Branch

managers were targeted on revenue. They allocated work to installation schedules according to its contribution to their budget, not commitments already made to customers. When the engineers arrived on site they would often have to redo the salesperson's work; they might have to ask the customer about the siting of equipment or would have to return for more equipment.

You will recall that the customer parted with half of the payment at the time of sale. The second payment was triggered by the original installation date. Delays to the installation schedule caused by a branch manager's attention to revenue meant that some customers would receive a demand for the second payment before installation. This was the biggest cause of customer complaints. Documenting the procedures of this system will not have improved anything, and it might have made things worse.

The organisation on which this example is based was registered to ISO 9000; it had to be to satisfy the requirements of its industry regulator. The ISO 9000 defenders might argue that, for example, keeping the salespeople "controlled" by administration refusing to accept uncompleted or inaccurate forms will improve things. In our experience it only leads to increased conflict between administration and sales (and did so in this case); it is no more than an attempt to control symptoms — to deal with problems caused by the system. The causes of failure we have identified so far were mostly due to the way the organisation used measures. They were used to monitor and control functions; weekly reports would show numbers for revenue and costs. It may have come to the reader's attention that they were not really achieving control in terms of what was happening for the customer. The system's failures were, quite naturally, causing more demands from its customers — customers were progress-chasing and complaining. To establish a set of procedures for handling customer complaints (a favourite demand of ISO 9000 assessors) would only miss the point — all of this dysfunctional activity was caused by the way the organisation worked. The priority has to be to change the way it works. To reveal the failures one has to look outside-in, one has to see how the parts worked together. It is axiomatic to a systems perspective that it would be more efficient and better for future revenues to make and meet commitment to customers, to agree and deliver without causing waste. Implementing ISO 9000 had only served to "lock in" waste.

> An administration division of a life insurance company received a lot of calls from the field sales force. The sales force was unhappy about how quickly the calls were handled. The organisation had (foolishly)[3] introduced service standards but they were not being met. A meeting was organised between the managers from sales and administration. The sales managers argued that the solution would be to create a "one-stop shop", a call-handling unit which would take responsibility for all calls and answer them immediately. In that way, they argued, the calls would not be an interruption to the administrative work. (An interesting assumption, given that dealing with calls did constitute a lot of the work. While it might be plausible to assume that administrators should simply process papers, to do so currently required interactions between sales and administration. This was a feature of the way the system currently worked.) The administration managers argued that a "one-stop shop" was impractical and that it would be better to use the established "experts" to answer calls, as they are the ones who knew the answers. There was an impasse. Two strongly held opinions.

The administration department was registered to ISO 9000. People worked to procedures. No one had thought to measure anything, to understand what was going on. What was the volume of calls coming in? How predictable was it? What types of calls came in and how predictable was each type? How long (predictably) did it take to handle the different types of calls? Were some more time-consuming than others? How many of the

---

[3] To establish a service standard without first establishing capability is gambling with two possibilities: first, that the standard is beyond the current capability and will not be met, causing distortion and complaints; second, that the standard is below current capability, being easily met and thus putting an artificial ceiling on performance — see below.

calls coming in were calls which were caused by a failure of the system which, in an ideal world, should be eradicated? In other words, what can we learn about the predictability of demand and the predictability of response? And what could we learn about the way the system responds? How well does it respond to customers from the customers' point of view and how efficiently does it respond to the various types of demand? These are the data that would illuminate the means for improvement; they would tell us about what the system is doing. To act on these data would improve service and reduce costs. Implementing ISO 9000 merely served to prevent people taking such a perspective.

Managing a system requires data about demand and flow

Without data about demand and flow, management can only rely on opinion to make decisions. In the above example, if the opinion of the salespeople had prevailed, people in administration would look for evidence that it was the wrong thing to do (and vice-versa). The data required for informed decision-making were beyond the view of these managers. Managers measured staff activity in administration (transactions handled) and complaints; their preoccupation was to get staff to "do more" and "do better", whereas a systems view would have provided the means to achieve these ends. Acting on the measures they had could only make things worse. If the managers had known what was predictable about demand and flow, they could have agreed upon a new way of working, against which they could have tested their assumptions. They would have been learning rather than trading opinions.

Improvement starts with understanding variation

To work with the notion of predictability, managers need to know about the theory of variation. Deming compared ISO 9000 and the theory of variation in one of his last interviews (*Industry Week*, January 1994):

"ISO 9000, 9001, 9002 are conformance specifications — conform to requirements. But that's not enough; that won't do it. One must seek the nominal value[4] of anything, what the best way is, not just pass the course. To meet specifications, do what is required — that is not enough. You have to do better than that. Achieve uniformity about the nominal value, best value. Shrink, shrink, shrink variation about the nominal value. That is where you get your payoff; that is where you get ahead."

Managers have grown up in a world dominated by the ideas of "conformance to specifications" or "working to standards". Henry Ford showed the world what could be achieved by standardisation. He reduced the cost of motor vehicle manufacturing and, as a consequence, made motor transportation accessible to the mass market. Ford brought the world the benefits of mass production and it became the model of "good" management. The ideas spread from manufacturing to service organisations. Work could be managed if it is broken down into parts and those parts are measured for cost-effectiveness. The key to mass production was standardisation of parts and their assembly; no longer was there a need for fitters (workers who literally "fitted" parts by machining each to fit); manufacturing became assembly. The consequences of Ford's innovation are still evident today. Model T's in auction rooms often have components from different manufacturing years. One example can consist of parts which span 30 years of manufacturing history.

But standardisation is less than optimisation, as the Japanese were to discover. When work is made to a standard, variation remains. In assembled products, not all parts work together in exactly the same way. Variation in parts leads to exponentially increasing variation in the whole system, increasing the likelihood of failure. It was for this reason that the early motor manufacturing processes required huge "finishing" operations and, for example, early cars required drivers to be mechanics. Despite the overall improvements in automotive product qual-

---

[4] Nominal value is explained below.

ity, such differences still exist between manufacturers. Some manufacturers' finishing costs have been reported to be more than others' original manufacturing costs.[5]

Ko Yoshida, a Japanese academic and management consultant based in the US, calls working to standards "acceptability quality":

> "If you are working on acceptability concepts, that is the quickest way to bankrupt your company" (Ko Yoshida, 1996 speech to the British Deming Association).

Standards are a compromise, but the idea of using standards is deeply ingrained in the traditional manager's psyche. They seek to protect a manufacturing process from only the extremes of variation. Components made to a standard are judged to be acceptable if they fall between acceptable limits (see Figure 5.3). It was Taguchi who first showed the superiority of working to reduce variation. Rather than produce parts within acceptable limits — to a standard — he showed that it was far better to choose any point on the continuum (making this the nominal value) and make parts more and more alike. As variation between parts is reduced, in whatever small amounts, the variation in the whole system reduces and thus decreases the likelihood of failure. In simple terms, this is why Japanese cars have become more and more reliable.

Figure 5.3 Make to Standards vs Reduce Variation

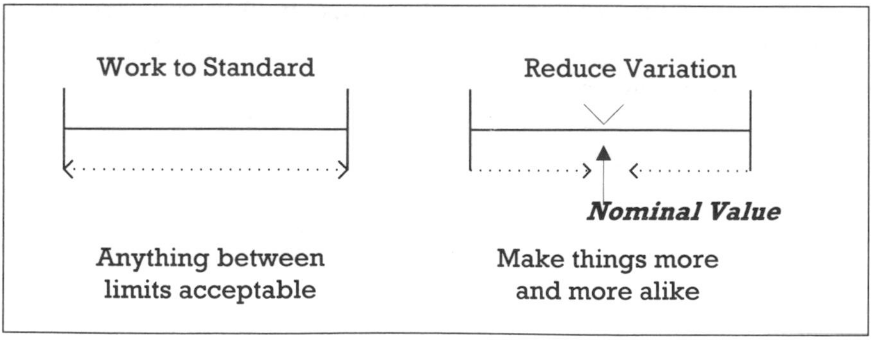

---

[5] See *The Machine that Changed the World*, Womack, Roos and Jones, Harper Collins, 1991.

An American motor manufacturer opened a transmissions plant in Japan. After a few years, the American transmissions plant managers noticed that their Japanese counterparts were making transmissions which broke down a lot less (in fact, hardly ever). What action did they take? True to a red-blooded, competitive mentality, the Americans bought a transmission which had been manufactured by the Japanese. A co-operative response might have been to pick up the telephone and ask what they were doing.

The Americans took the Japanese transmission apart and measured its components. To their surprise, the components did not show the expected "tolerances" or variation. Perturbed, they sent their measuring equipment away for re-calibration, assuming it was faulty — they could have easily checked their equipment by taking one of their own transmissions from the line. There were no "tolerances" (expected variations) in the Japanese transmission.

It is axiomatic that there will always be variation. No two tasks are the same, no two days are the same. Managers ignore variation at their peril.

There are two types of variation, "common-cause" and "special-cause". In simple terms,[6] if measures taken over time are plotted in a control chart and all values fall between the upper and lower control limits (UCL and LCL), it can be said that all variation is due to "common causes" (see Figure 5.4).

"Common causes" are causes within the system; without action on the system we can expect performance to continue to be between the two limits on the control chart. The limits on a control chart, determined statistically, show what possible values can be expected to be produced by a process or system given the variation in observations taken over time. "Special-cause" variation describes events that fall outside the control limits. They are due to a special event, possibly a "one-off". The value suggests that statistically this cannot be attributed to the same process or system — something extraordinary has happened.

---

[6] This explanation is not strictly true but sufficient for our purposes here; for a more thorough explanation of learning from variation go to www.lean-service.com

Figure 5.4 Common Cause and Special Cause Variation

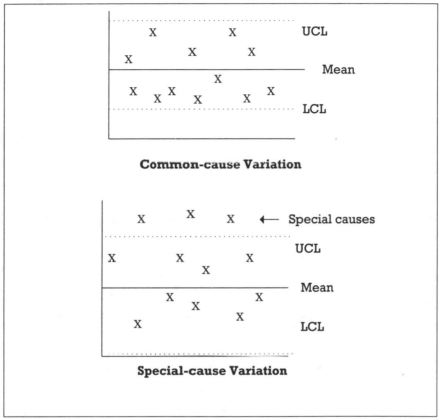

The distinction between "common-cause" and "special-cause" helps managers avoid making decisions that make matters worse. In our experience the most common fault in management decision-making is reacting to a "signal" which is not there — in other words treating "common-cause" variation as though it is "special-cause". It is an understandable error. In real terms a number has gone up or down and the manager feels obliged to respond. But in practice his response might only increase variation; he might put in a new procedure or change a policy which only makes things worse.

If a work standard is set at a level beyond the system or process capability (see Figure 5.5), then nothing other than "cheating" will ensure that people avoid getting grief from their managers.

Figure 5.5 Standard Exceeds Capability

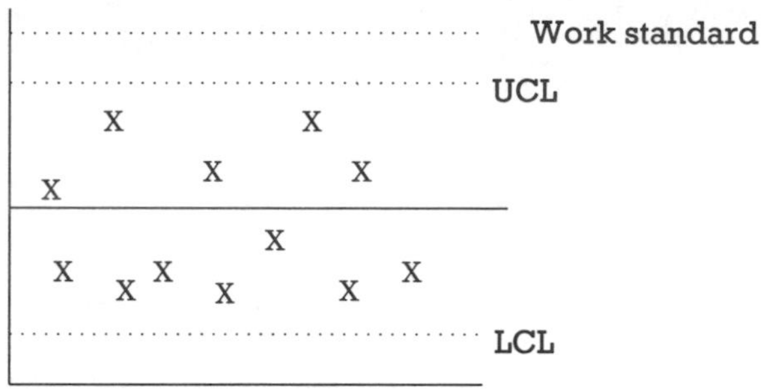

If a work standard is set at a level which is easily achieved by the process capability (see Figure 5.6), there is no incentive to work for improvement; people slow down. In either case, the work ethic becomes "get to the standard", do whatever it takes to avoid negative consequences (being "paid attention to"). In human terms, this is no different from the experience of being "assessed" against ISO 9000. The anticipation of inspection of one's work by others will encourage anyone to do whatever they have to do to be seen to conform. In this way, ISO 9000 assessment, just like "management by the numbers", can cause distortion of a system or process, increasing variation — people doing whatever is required to pass inspection (for instance, ensuring that the paperwork is up-to date, being seen to be applying unnecessary controls, hiding things) regardless of the impact on the service and efficiency of their business.

When people are required to work to standards the result is often demoralisation. If the standard is *within* the limits of "natural" (i.e. system-induced) variation (see Figure 5.7), some days workers will be "winners" — they will meet or exceed the standard — and some days they will be "losers". It is inevitable because their performance is governed by variation in the system.

It is management's task to understand and act on the causes of variation. Learning from variation is fundamental to continuous improvement.

Figure 5.6 Standard Less than Capability

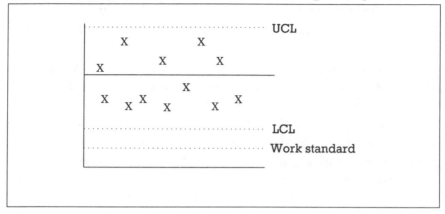

Figure 5.7 Some Days You Win, Some Days You Lose

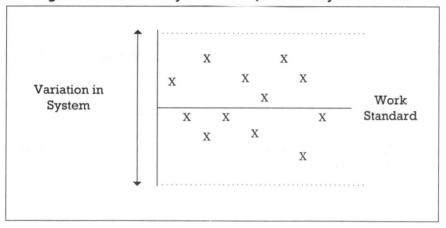

In his famous four-day seminars, Deming would conduct what he called the "red beads experiment". He would ask for volunteers ("willing workers"), show them their task and then allow them to perform a series of trials. The task was to take a paddle, which had fifty holes in it, and place it in a box containing mostly white beads and a few red ones. The object was to "get white beads", which of course was almost impossible because a few red ones would always creep in.

Deming would amuse his audience by behaving as a manager would. He would give a demonstration and make it the "work standard" — "If I can do it, so can you". He would repeatedly proclaim that the customer wanted white beads (and would tolerate just a few red ones, as achieved in the work standard). He would praise those workers who achieved the work standard or better — "Good work, you'll go far". He would punish those who fell below the standard — "Sloppy, try harder" and so on. After a training trial and a couple of work trials, Deming (as the boss) would sack those who had consistently under-performed ("We'll keep just the good workers — that way we'll get more of what we want"). Of course, in subsequent trials, some of the "good workers" also "failed".

It was a simple exercise with a profound point. People's performance is governed by their system. Nothing would change the fact that there were "red beads" in the system. It is the nature of "red beads" that they affect performance differently on different occasions.

To get an idea of the impact of "red beads" on performance, we often encourage managers to do as Deming did in his experiment — plot the performance of workers over time. In other words, make a control chart. If, as is so often the case, performance shows variation but is "in control" (i.e. predictable), then they can start working with their people on the causes of variation. To ignore the causes of variation ("red beads") and to rate worker against worker (with no evidence to show that the differences are real) is a sure way to demoralise people.

> A telemarketing team was measured on number of calls, contacts, and "sends" (a sale subject to trial). Daily and weekly targets were set. Achieving target resulted in a bonus. Managers foolishly praised and paid those who made their target and "coached" or "paid attention to" those who did not. The people were demoralised. Roughly two days in any week they had to experience going home having failed to meet their target, yet they had been as busy as ever. They knew in their hearts they had done their best. However, their performance was governed by the system. Plotting performance on a control chart showed that their performance was predictable; differences were due to common-cause variation, there was little any individual could do to improve performance (see Figure 5.8). On investigation it

was revealed that the single largest cause of variation was the quality of the prospect lists. Lists had duplications, the remains of partially used lists were kept in people's drawers, stored for re-use when nothing else was available. As all lists came from the same source this resulted in waste. Customers were being re-called frequently (generating complaints), errors in the lists were being found more than once, some customers (at the back end of lists) would never get called. The second largest cause of variation was product knowledge, which varied extensively between operators. Other sources of variation were the time taken to process orders because some depended on other departments, the type of product, and the fact that there were frequent "fire-fighting" interruptions to the working day.

Figure 5.8 Telemarketing Performance is Stable — Variation is Common Cause

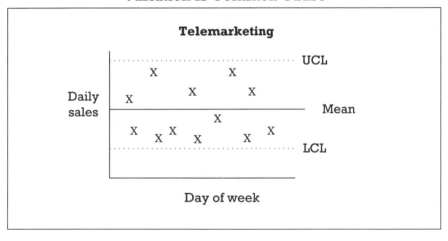

People learned to do whatever they had to do to make their targets. They hid good quality lists, falsified activity records, "bounced" incoming customer calls to others so as not to get tied up with a customer problem, sent goods "on approval" in the knowledge that customers would return them and so on. They were not bad people, they were working in a bad system.

The performance of this system didn't depend on how the parts act independently (getting lists made "on time" and meeting activity targets for calls — the measures preoccupying managers), it depended on how the parts worked together. It is management's role to manage the interactions (or system), not to manage activity. Being clear about the purpose of the system and measuring performance in relation to purpose over time (to establish the extent of variation) are the first steps. Only attention to the causes of variation would result in improved performance. Improving the quality of lists, increasing the product knowledge of operators and removing the causes of customer problem-calls would improve performance. It is not unusual to find such "traditionally managed" telemarketing systems under-performing by half.

Management, assuming that differences in performance were attributable to differences between people, saw their job as "motivating" people — "get people to make more calls". The managers assumed people to be motivated by targets and bonuses, yet they presided over a system where the success of any particular call was beyond the control of their people. In such conditions people do whatever it takes to get the bonus, but they "know" they are at the mercy of the system. It is very demoralising to work under such conditions; the task loses its intrinsic value. Pride, the most important source of motivation, is lost.

Coming to terms with how the current system causes sub-optimisation is a powerful way of learning — it is important to learn why something is wrong as well as simply that it is wrong. Managers who rely on measures of activity to manage productivity recognise the need to abandon them when they understand just how such measures are actually damaging productivity. They abandon them with confidence when they know which measures to use instead — that is, measures which relate to purpose — and they know how best to use them — that is, to learn from variation. ISO 9000 teaches managers nothing about any of this. If anything, it prevents such discussions even getting onto the table because of its approach to implementation and the contents of its clauses

The capability of a process or system can be easily established by plotting its performance over time and determining, through statistical methods, what the process or system will predictably achieve while advancing, providing there are no substantive changes.[7]

The principles associated with reducing variation apply equally to manufacturing and service organisations, but there are important differences as to how they should be applied, as we shall demonstrate.

> "To gain customer trust, the variation of service must be reduced" (Ko Yoshida, 1996 speech to the British Deming Association).

Starting from this assertion, one can take either of two routes. The first would be to standardise service — the assumption being that customers' expectations will be managed by providing the same service anywhere in the world. The second route is to design the organisation to be customer-shaped — to respond to their particular need in a way which suits the particular circumstances. The question is: who sets the "nominal value"?

The McDonald's fast-food restaurant chain is the classic example of the first route. The organisation has set the nominal value. But it does not follow that standardisation is always equivalent to excellent service. It was obvious to Ray Kroc, at that time a soft drinks salesman, that the McDonald's brothers' restaurant in Boston was a success. It was his idea to replicate the formula so that he could (as a supplier) do more business. The McDonald brothers gave him the right to franchise their idea and the rest, as they say, is history. That McDonald's has been a success is of no doubt, but it was an idea which was "tested" before being replicated — the evidence was that they had hit upon a "nominal value" that appealed to many.

However, there are many people who will not go into a McDonald's. McDonald's represents a standard offering that is the nominal value for many (but not all) people — they know it and they like it. Managers, seeing the success of McDonald's, tend to argue for standardisation of service. We often hear international managers say they want their operations to have

---

[7] For more information on the use of measures in decision-making, visit www.lean-service.com

the same "look and feel" wherever they exist. It is more important to know what works — what matters to customers and how well you work in that regard. Indeed, it is vital to know what works before it is replicated across many sites, lest you replicate sub-optimisation. The replication of the McDonald's formula was not standardisation for standardisation's sake.

In service organisations, the customer sets the nominal value

Service organisations differ from manufacturing organisations. Service is created at the moment of transaction. To apply Taguchi's thinking to service organisations requires a different way of thinking about his principle. It is the customer who sets the nominal value. The organisation should be designed to allow the customer to "pull value" from it at the point of transaction. Any departure from the customer's "nominal value" risks economic loss.

When the service organisation sets the nominal value it will increase the probability of economic loss. This is why service standards and guarantees have been a failure. To take an example:

> The customers of a country roadside restaurant may all have a different "nominal value". Fishermen arriving at six in the morning will want service delivered differently from a family who arrive in the mid-afternoon. A businesswoman with a laptop computer will have yet a different view of what would constitute good service for her. The managers of such organisations often mistakenly set work standards and procedures which effectively guarantee poor service to a high proportion of their customers. Typically, they specify how the customer should be greeted, seated and in what order things should happen. Any member of staff caught "breaking the rules" is subject to disciplinary action. A recipe for demoralisation.

Managers establish such systems because they believe it makes the organisation easy to manage. Management becomes specifying what people should do and checking that people are working to that way. In recent years, these organisations have begun to get their customers to control service agent behaviour. They offer the customer free "upgrades" or "extras" if the customers can catch the agent doing something "wrong". This may, for some agents, be fun at first, but it can only lead to demoralisation.

"Catching people doing things wrong" has led to the rise of a new service called "mystery shopping". A mystery shopper is someone who pretends to be a customer, visiting a retail outlet or calling a telephone service with a "tick-sheet" and recording the behaviour of the service agent. Managers are told that this data will be usable for improvement. Yet they cannot be; they only measure the mechanics of a transaction — did he or she smile, offer an alternative and so on. In practice, they can only be used to issue edicts and if the required behaviour increases variation, worsening performance, the managers never know. We recommend our clients to avoid wasting money on mystery shopping; we have found that mystery shopping always causes sub-optimisation of performance. Two examples:

> In a telephone-based travel service, service agents had always been able to establish whether callers were bona fide members and thus entitled to the service. Non-members would politely be advised to try a good alternative. Managers employed mystery shoppers to "control" the behaviour of service agents. The agents would not dare deal with anyone who was not a member in their usual way just in case the caller was a mystery shopper. As a consequence, time to handle calls went up, productivity went down.

> A salesman in a car retailer picked up the telephone and perceptibly changed his demeanour. He sat down, took out a manual from his desk drawer and proceeded to deal with a lengthy conversation. On finishing we asked what had been going on. "That was a mystery shopper," we were told. "You can always tell, they ask questions that normal customers don't ask." He explained that the manufacturers used mystery shopping to determine a service score for retailers and that score would determine the retailer's bo-

nus. In the time that he was on the telephone a number of potential customers went through his shop. It was economically more advantageous for him to deal with the mystery shopper than to service customers.

In every case we have studied we have found mystery shopping to be inhibiting performance. In one case we were surprised to hear that people liked mystery shopping but in fact they liked it only because it was their only form of feedback. They had fun "turning it on" for the mystery shopper and getting good scores on their report.

Mystery shopping finds a market amongst those managers who believe in standardisation. They see their job as determining what people should do at the point of service, issuing service standards, prescriptions and scripts. These things may or may not create value for customers, but in practice will always result in customer dissatisfaction at some level simply because the organisation has set the "nominal value". Customers want service to be customer-shaped.

Rather than specify service it is far better to ask: "what do we know about the predictability of demand and how does this system respond to demand?" Implicit in any demand is the "nominal value" — what the customer needs or wants and what would create value for the customer. The further the response is from the customer's need (variation), the greater the economic loss.

The system governs behaviour

The compartmentalisation logic of "command and control" thinking is not limited to the design of organisation structures. A systems view of organisations shows the fallacy of conceptualising performance problems as people problems ("if only they would do it"). Failures in co-operation, poor morale and conflicts in our organisations are symptoms; they should not be considered separately from an understanding of the system. When they are, and are "treated" with training, the training usually does no more than treat the symptoms while the causes remain. Managers have been encouraged to think of the "human" (or "soft") issues as distinct from "hard" or "task" issues when the two would be better understood as interdependent. Empowerment is a preoccupation of "command and control" managers, but they fail to see that they have created systems which disempower people. It is only when a person's view of how to do work, how to understand it, control it and improve it changes that their behaviour changes. Changing the system begins with thinking differently.

ISO 9000 is not different thinking. It imparts a philosophy of controlling people's behaviour through procedures, forms and documentation. The assumption is that people need to be controlled. "Command and control" management thinking began with the separation of decision-making from doing. ISO 9000 was originally conceived when such doctrine was the norm — a norm which managers are only now beginning to question. ISO 9000 was a solution to problems which themselves were products of the same thinking — "why won't people do as they are told?" Controlling people's behaviour had, and continues to have, some success at tackling symptoms, but it fails to focus attention on the systemic causes — "why do people do as they do?"

Control of people's behaviour through procedures at best controls output, that is, by making output consistent (whether good or bad). This is why it is true to claim that an organisation can be registered to ISO 9000 and deliver poor quality (consistently). We do not argue that procedures are never helpful (although they are unhelpful in many circumstances); our argument is that starting from an attitude of "control" prevents managers taking the opportunity to learn and improve, as we shall see in each of the case studies (in Chapter 6).

High-performance organisations give control to the people who do the work — they are in control, not being controlled. The measures which are needed in such circumstances are not measures of conformance to procedures, or attainment of "traditional" output measures — for they afford no control, they only tell you what has happened. The measures required are those which illuminate what is going on in the system. In the examples we have used here the vital system measures were ones of demand and response. In order to learn, these measures need to be plotted in control charts, as under-standing the predictability of demand or response and the nature and causes of variation would lead to learning and improvement.

Improvement begins with understanding the organisation as a system

To understand the organisation as a system is to see two things: the scope for potential improvement — what it could look like — and the means or leverage for change. Changing the system usually means taking out things which have been limiting or damaging current performance, for example, removing activity measures, arbitrary targets or standards and ceasing to manage performance through budgets — in other words, changing structures, information and processes to enable the whole to better achieve its purpose. Managers will only take such radical action if and when they appreciate that their traditional means of control in fact give them less control: managing costs produces more costs. When managers understand their organisation as a system, the inappropriateness of traditional practices becomes stark. It is a major source of motivation for action. Action means "doing the right thing", putting in place the right system to ensure that performance is managed against purpose, and managed from a strong base of understanding.

In our experience, organisations registering to ISO 9000 show little such understanding of their current organisation as a system, and the experience of registration only prevents them from taking such a view. In every organisation we have studied the first steps to registration were documenting procedures according to the prescription and creating a bureaucracy for their "management". The meaning of "continuous improvement" in such circumstances is no more than "improve through thinking of a better procedure": it is not a way of thinking which is underpinned by an understanding of the organisation as a system and how to manage through measuring and learning from variation.

Taking a systems approach to software quality ("Tickit"): An illustration

As early as the mid-1980s, the UK government was aware of the widespread disaffection with what was then BS 5750 (the reader might reflect on how the bandwagon rolled on to create ISO 9000 in spite of the well-known problems). Rather than call a halt the decision was made to improve in one sector. This resulted in the birth of "Tickit", which is ISO 9000 for software development organisations. This is how a correspondent put it to us:

> "There had been a lot of questions and concerns about assessors. It was obvious that we needed better ones, but to try to control what had become a burgeoning population would be difficult, if not impossible. The answer was to try to improve the quality of assessing in just one sector and the IT sector was chosen because everybody expressed concerns about the performance of software products and the potential gains from quality improvement in software products were significant. The revisionists argued that assessors should not be full-time appointments (to get away from the 'surplus Government inspectors') but instead should be employed on a part-time basis, using people with jobs in the particular industry. At this time there were other problems that needed to be solved. BSI (British Standards Institution) had the lion's share of the assessment market in the UK and had the advantage of being associated with the 'kite mark', something people were familiar with as it had been applied to products for generations; it was not easy for new entrants to get established in the assessment business. Creating another 'mark' could solve the problem. Tickit represented a 'better' accreditation scheme, designed to exert better control of the assessing organisations. Auditors had to meet strict criteria, had to complete a specific course relating to ISO 9000 assessment in the IT sector and were selected by a panel. The Tickit scheme published a customer guide (what you can expect from ISO 9000), a supplier guide (how to conduct ISO 9000 for your software organisation), and an auditor's guide designed to encourage consistency of auditing.
>
> In addition, the Tickit scheme included three-yearly complete audits, a change from the usual practice where, once

registered, an organisation only experiences part-audits.
Needing to undertake a full review every three years, it was
felt, would precipitate greater competition in the market as
organisations would be more likely to shop around for assessors. In truth, and if it works, all Tickit represents is a
better application of ISO 9000."

An unanticipated consequence of Tickit has been discontent at
the rule that organisations producing software must be assessed through the Tickit scheme. As more and more products
include software, the non-Tickit assessing organisations are
getting uncomfortable. They are seeing themselves being
squeezed out of their markets.

But has Tickit solved the problem? We have had a number of
experiences with software companies that have shown us that
Tickit has the same problems as ISO 9000. Here is a solution we
have found to be of value to software companies struggling with
what to do about Tickit. This solution is based on a systems approach and applies to any organisation where everything that is
made is a "one-off". But first the presenting problem:

ISO 9000 registration resulted in procedures that were perceived by software engineers as a chore and a constraint — the
procedures did not suit the variety of tasks. As a first step, the
engineers looked at their organisation as a system to understand the what and why of current performance. Analysis of
customer demand showed the variety of things customers
wanted to meet their business needs. Analysis of value showed
how value work was predictably fragmented by the current
work procedures. Analysis of flow showed predictable volumes
of waste.

The solution was simple but profoundly different. While all
customer demands differed, at the highest level all demand
went through four stages: understand the customer's nominal
value (what matters to the customer), plan a method, do the
work, review the work against chosen measures. At each stage
the best methods would vary. For example, establishing the
nominal value for a technical report would require completely
different methods from establishing the nominal value for a new
piece of software. The answer was to locate the variety of "ex-

pertise" outside the four main stages in a new quality management system. The responsibility of any project manager was now to determine what "expertise" to "pull" in to the flow at each stage. Not only did this return control of the work to the project managers, it led workers to value depositing knowledge in the management system, for previous experience now had value in solving today's problems.

Instead of being "controlled by procedures", the engineers were now "in control" of the work. Rather than waste being caused by unnecessary bureaucracy, waste was deigned out by focusing on how to do the value work for any particular customer demand.

In every case where we have helped implement such a solution we have had to train the ISO 9000 assessor in how to inspect it. The written documentation — the usual starting-place for inspection — is minimal. Inspection of this system requires asking questions about the work, to ask of any project manager: "What is this project? What stage are you at? Have you satisfied the principles at each stage and how? What have you chosen to 'pull' in doing so?"

Many inspectors are more comfortable working from documentation. But all who have been shown this approach have been happy to follow these principles. Perhaps this reflects the assessors' need to keep the business. What is important, however, is that neither ISO 9000 registration nor assessor advice led these organisations to a systems solution.

Systems thinking is simple but different

The systems solution is based on ideas developed by the leading quality thinkers. If these leaders could communicate a way of looking at and improving work to a group of Japanese industrialists who got results in a relatively short time, it begs the question: Is ISO 9000 communicating badly or communicating the wrong thing? The leaders of the quality movement did not communicate a prescription, but rather a way of thinking. The consequences were a different approach to the design and management of work that led to learning and improvement.

To manage an organisation as a system was and is a better solution. It is a view which is diametrically opposed to traditional "command and control" thinking; the view we took when we studied the cases which are the subject of our next chapter.

Chapter 6

ISO 9000 CASE STUDIES

In seeking to understand what ISO 9000 registration meant for organisation performance, we learned that opinion surveys were unreliable. Those who had reported positive results were often unaware of the practical evidence to the contrary within their organisations. Examples of problems associated with ISO 9000 registration were everywhere. There were very few outside of the ISO 9000 movement who would claim ISO 9000 to be a positive contribution to organisation performance; but we still knew little about what had happened in our organisations and on what scale. Was ISO 9000 contributing to performance in any respect, and if so where and how? Were the much talked-of problems isolated or common? Nobody knew. We needed to learn more about what would predictably happen to an organisation if it registered to ISO 9000. We needed to learn about cause and effect, so we turned to conducting case studies.

Some people might feel that case studies would not be representative. But we would ask the reader to consider the following argument: if one were to find examples of practice in organisations which were specifically linked to registration to ISO 9000, one could predict that others were likely to do the same. To be satisfied of the probability that others would do likewise, one would have to show how the practices were caused by the Standard (i.e. related to its clauses) and its associated system (i.e. the recommended method of implementation, the advice of assessors, marketplace coercion, managers who did not understand). If there are predictive links we should expect to find that many of the problems associated with ISO 9000 registration are common to registered organisations.

As we shall show, sub-optimisation associated with registration to ISO 9000 goes beyond the well-known problems of bureaucratisation. Organisations are making themselves less easy to do business with, often increasing their costs and, most important of all, as the management ideas associated with ISO 9000 gain acceptance as the "proper way" to do business, organisations are blinding themselves to the means by which they might otherwise improve. In the majority of the cases we report here the companies felt that ISO 9000 registration had been beneficial.

TECH. CO.

. . . controlling sales and putting customers in their place

Background

"Tech. Co." is a sales and distribution organisation based in the UK. All products sold by the company are manufactured by its parent company overseas. The products are high-technology products sold to business and government customers. Tech. Co. decided to register to ISO 9000 in 1993. The primary reason for seeking registration was that Government customers were insisting on it. It was also felt that the company might achieve some benefits from clarity of working procedures. Originally the company had seven divisions (organised by product) and each division had its own sales order function. It had recently centralised the sales order functions — in a structural sense — but the people who worked within product divisions still processed orders for the same products. The primary change with centralisation was standardisation of working procedures. Tech. Co. took advice from a consultant. The work to first registration took three years and registration was successful.

Registration to ISO 9000 meant the creation of nine manuals of procedures. One for the overall management system, one for each type of product and one for the warehouse. The manuals documented what should be done at each stage of an order; nothing had been left out. The quality manager took the view that sales administration was now controlled. The standard procedures meant that people would not get things wrong. He also viewed salespeople as needing to be controlled: "They won't be able to get away with giving administrators inadequate information and what they provide has to be written down." He also saw advantages in controlling customers: "Because we have controlled procedures we can prove to them what they have ordered if there is any dispute."

How had ISO 9000 contributed to performance?

The first operational problems were felt by sales. The attitude presented to them by administration was that "nothing proceeds without the right paperwork".

There had been a cultural tradition of salespeople being "heroes". Sales people had treated "back office" staff work as drudgery, were always seeking last-minute changes to orders and were rarely accurate with their form-filling. But now administration had been instructed to work to procedures. Some agreed with the quality manager that working to procedures would teach salespeople to pay more attention to putting the right information on their paperwork, but sales peoples' behaviour did not change. The same conflicts existed between sales and administration; indeed, they were sometimes more acute because administration now had a specific stick with which to beat the salespeople.

The causes of these conflicts were many, but the one cause that appeared to be having the most influence was the complexity of pricing. Salespeople faced a variety of different circumstances when contracting with customers; the organisation needed flexible administrative practices. The complexity of current practices had been documented in the manuals. It would be unlikely that an administrator would be familiar with all situations and, furthermore, the manual would be unlikely to cover all situations (without being continually up-dated). The consequences were an increasing sense of drudgery amongst administrators and none of the original problems were solved.

The problem in administration was compounded by the way the new procedures had been introduced (it was said that they were "dumped" on administrative staff with the directive "you are to work to these procedures"). The attitude in administration soon became "work to procedures" rather than serve customers. Furthermore, it was a perspective that valued working to procedures above finding and removing errors or the causes of errors. When asked whether the new procedures had improved performance, no one could say. There had been no collection of data on the performance of the administrative practices prior to the new procedures and hence it was not possible to determine whether things were better or worse.

The administration manager's attitude to customers ("the procedures will enable us to prove what the customer ordered if there is a dispute") was positively dangerous. What matters when a customer disputes, or for any reason wants a change to an order, is that the need is dealt with promptly and courteously. The last thing the customer wants to hear is someone seeking to prove them wrong.

The Standard requires control of returned goods. The way this was implemented in Tech. Co. was revealing. The volume of goods returned stayed at the same level as prior to registration (suggesting no change to the performance of the system). What did change was the way returned goods were handled, because of the requirement to control product which is returned by customers ("control of non-conforming product"). All goods returned by customers were now held in "quarantine", pending authorisation for release into the warehouse (for reuse). There had been considerable debate about what to do with returned product. Tech. Co.'s products were sensitive to excesses of temperature and light. If they had been subjected to adverse conditions while on the customers' premises they would be ruined. If product was tested on return it would be destroyed — the nature of the product precluded testing (or sampling). The choice was simple: return product to the warehouse or destroy it.

In the event, a compromise was developed. It was argued that product returned within 15 days would be unlikely to have

been subjected to adverse conditions. The procedure for returned product required the warehouse supervisor to check
date of receipt against date of despatch and, where it fitted the
new rule, to send a list of returned product to a director for signature. Signatories were hard to find. When they were available, they were not inclined to treat signing forms from the
warehouse as their top priority.

But nobody asked the question "what data are there about
the nature and causes of returns?" with a view to eradicating the
problem. And, more importantly, nobody had asked the question "have we ever had a problem with product being returned
and then sent out on another order?" The answer, when asked,
was "no". There had been no need to create this "quarantine"
procedure. It would have been perfectly in order to have
placed all returned goods in inventory. All of the available evidence showed that there was not a problem. Because of the
Standard's requirement Tech. Co. had set up a procedure for an
uncommon occurrence (special cause) assuming it to be a
common occurrence (common cause) and had created a whole
new set of problems. The result was losses to the system. At the
time of this study, product to the value of half a million pounds
was not available for sale.

If they had viewed their organisation as a system, and had
measured the right things, they would have known that returned product had not shown signs of fault and would have
recognised that customers in receipt of faulty goods were a rar-
ity. In the improbable event of a customer receiving faulty
goods, the organisation could respond by engaging in excellent "repair" — give the customers whatever was necessary to
solve their problem and create value for them. A good way to
show what matters and a better procedure, given the evidence.

There is little that can be said in support of the view that ISO
9000 contributed to improving organisational performance in
this case. It seems the implicit purpose of registration was to
create a "control through procedures system", rather than help
the business. It might have been labelled a "quality system" but
its features were hardly promoting quality. The emphasis on
written work procedures was entirely unnecessary — a simple

flow chart would have been sufficient (and may have been of more use in clarifying purpose). The manuals produced for administration should not have been necessary. If they had a purpose at all they should have been used for job training. Used in the way they were only exacerbated the problems between sales and administration.

This was a classic "bomb factory" approach to ISO 9000 implementation. The purpose of this organisation is to distribute product in the UK, that is, to sell. How should it do that, by what method? By creating value for customers, developing loyal customers, attending to customers' needs. Nothing was being done to understand and improve the core processes of achieving the organisation's purpose. ISO 9000 was making achievement of the purpose more difficult and more expensive.

METAL CO.

. . . if you don't comply, we won't buy

"Metal Co." is a supplier of processed metals to manufacturing organisations. Like many other organisations, in the late 1980s they had experienced a high volume of questionnaires from customers wanting to know about their quality management system. The management felt that if they achieved registration to ISO 9000, this would satisfy their customers' requirements.

Conscious of the dangers of over-bureaucratisation, the chief executive appointed a quality manager, chosen because he had successfully taken two other companies through registration. The quality manager applied for assessment against the Standard immediately on appointment. He knew that there was a waiting period of about six months (because of demand) and he wanted to set clear expectations amongst Metal Co.'s employees. His recent experience had taught him that enthusiasm for the Standard easily waned. To quote him:

> "I learned that if you give someone something to do and there is no value in it, they lose interest in it."

There was no doubt in his mind, having been through the experience twice before, that the principle benefit of the Standard was, as he called it, "flag waving" — being able to show potential customers you were registered. We probed whether he really had such a jaundiced view and his response was:

> "Behind the scenes the Standard is an inhibitor; if you follow the rules it slows you down."

He gave us examples:

> "We had to demonstrate that instructions from sales to works were confirmed as correct. That meant the work instructions had to be signed. You were not allowed to have sales sign their own work, so works instructions would wait for signatures. To deal with the situation, people would 'cheat', they would simply take a bundle of instructions awaiting signature and sign them all."

You can imagine the impact on quality. A salesperson, knowing that their work was to be checked by someone else, would not be inclined to check it closely themselves. The person supposed to be checking would just sign them all off, assuming that the salespeople had done their job. No one was responsible, responsibility was shared. It is easy to see how inspection produces errors.

> "The amount of inspection required by the Standard was enormous. We had arguments with the assessors over "final inspection". Final inspection used to be the responsibility of the operator. Our process is quite simple: once a machine is set up, its performance shows minimal variation and all variation is always well within the specification. Hence inspection of the first and last piece made [by the operator] had always been satisfactory. The assessor wanted us to adopt a sampling plan, to sample pieces throughout the production run. There was no evidence that it was necessary, so we didn't — we just carried on as we always had but signed a form to say the work had been sampled. Furthermore, to do as the inspector had asked would have

slowed production because you cannot inspect while the machines are running."

If he had followed the advice of his assessor and stopped the production run, it might have resulted in what Deming called "tampering": taking actions which increased variation and made the process less reliable. But the assessor has power and it is interesting to note how some people deal with the power of the assessor — by giving up trying to fight it. Something else he said showed the peculiarity of the relationship between assessor and assessed:

> "Our lead assessor told us ISO 9000 is difficult to achieve but impossible to lose."

There was no doubt in his mind that the assessors meant that keeping the assessment was, from his point of view, the same as keeping the client. The assessor was just one component in the burden of being registered to ISO 9000:

> "The most time-consuming and wasteful consequence of registration has been the growth in paperwork. The primary need for paperwork is to show that you have followed procedures. It is there to enable the assessor to do his job. How else can you show conformance, other than through records?"

And the records required are pre-determined by what is written in the Standard. To take an example: the Standard requires documentary proof of the means by which the organisation approves suppliers. During an assessment the assessor had discovered that Metal Co. had been buying materials from an organisation which it had not formally "approved" as a supplier. The purchases were low-grade raw material, suitable for a variety of applications where the finished product was not going to be used for external or "visible" components; the characteristics of the materials were in no way deleteriously affecting the final product. This, in the quality manager's words, is what their assessor told them they should do:

> "He told us we should phone the customers whose supplies had included materials from these 'non-approved' suppliers and tell them so. Further, he said we should attach labels to all similar product leaving our premises to ensure that our customers knew their supplies were subject to non-approved raw materials."

Not only did this show a lack of common sense — the customers could not be adversely affected by the materials concerned — it showed a lack of commercial judgement. What did the assessor expect their customers to do in response to being sent such a warning? To avoid ever facing the same gruelling discussion about the extent to which this should matter, and to avoid ever having to upset customers in order to comply with the demands of an assessor, Metal Co. now pulls a list of suppliers off their purchasing database a week prior to assessment and presents this as the "approved supplier" list. It is a response to being "controlled" by their assessor; it does not reflect their attitude to working with suppliers. They are as determined as ever to work with their suppliers to improve quality.

Much of what we have reported so far can be readily found in a host of ISO 9000 registered companies. It was when the investigation turned to working with suppliers and customers that particularly interesting issues began to emerge. This was to see how ISO 9000 was affecting the whole "value chain" — everything from and to the paying customer. To quote the quality manager, firstly on managing suppliers:

> "To ensure supplier product meets requirements we have to take measures of all incoming product and plot it in SPC (statistical process control) charts. The suppliers have the same data but they won't release it to us because they feel it is 'company confidential'."

The consequence is waste; duplication of effort. More importantly, it is more likely to result in an adversarial relationship when discussing problems — "do my data agree with your data?" Suppliers who take the trouble to work with their customers learn more and improve their economic position. To understand how profound this is, we have to move to Metal Co.'s customers, one group of which understands this thinking. To spare their blushes, we have omitted the customers' names from the following startling revelation:

> "When supplying to (a British automotive company), they wanted to know whether we were registered to ISO 9000, it was a mandatory condition of doing business with them. Having achieved registration, they were satisfied. Now they only come and talk to us when something goes wrong. When supplying to (Japanese automotive company), they had no interest in whether we were registered to ISO 9000 and from day one of being a supplier, they were in our factory working with us on how our processes worked to supply theirs."

The Japanese had an attitude of "work in partnership, learn, improve". The following story illustrates the importance of attitude:

> A number of British organisations were competing to supply components to a Japanese manufacturer in the UK. Each had been asked to make a product according to a design. One had had a lot of problems and had been "back and forth" with trials, none of which had worked. It was this one which had won the contract. The managers were surprised, to say the least, as nothing they had supplied had worked. When they asked why they had won the contract they were told it was because they had the right attitude.

And what, by implication, was the attitude of the British automotive manufacturers being supplied by Metal Co.? Contractual, hands-off, controlling, even coercive. The "big three" American automotive manufacturers have taken this attitude one step further. Suppliers are being told that to do business they must be registered to QS 9000, a quality standard which goes further than ISO 9000 in that it gives more detailed specifications on how the ISO 9000 clauses should be interpreted and evidenced in practice. The president of one American manufacturer is reported to have said, "If you don't comply, we won't buy". But is he buying quality?

This is what Metal Co.'s quality manager told us about his Japanese customers in the UK:

> "They are not interested in ISO 9000, they are not interested in your organisation as such; but what they do take enormous interest in is what you do to make whatever you are supplying to them. They work with you to understand your process; to understand how your process is affecting their process. They will send their people to help and they expect you to think and work in the same way. They are not 'soft' about it, they expect you to take it as seriously as they do."

He followed his last point with a telling anecdote:

> "We made a small change to a part we were supplying to them, we changed a lubrication oil. After a few months they raised questions with us which showed they had noticed a change in the product at the time we made it and had been exploring the reasons why but had been unable to find out. When we disclosed what we had done they were furious. To them it was natural to communicate all changes, they thought about the work in process terms."

Metal Co. perceives their Japanese customers to have higher standards than their British customers, and their standards have nothing to do with ISO 9000. Yet the British and American automotive manufacturers think they are being tough in insisting on registration to ISO 9000. The American motor manufacturers' drive to oblige their suppliers to register to the even more demanding QS 9000 is just "more of the same". We think they are foolish rather than tough. The evidence points to the Japanese outperforming the Western motor manufacturers.[1] The difference is accounted for by attitude, and, moreover, method.

The difference starts with understanding and managing the organisation as a system. From this point of view, suppliers are part of the system, not merely "contractors". The Western

---

[1] See *The Machine that Changed the World*, Womack, Roos and Jones, Harper Collins, 1991.

manufacturers have realised, at least at a superficial level, that collaboration is important but their systems are designed to prevent it. The chief executive of Metal Co. illustrates the point:

> "One of the American manufacturers held an impressive 'road-show' with European suppliers. As well as explaining their new worldwide structure, their message was one of co-operation and partnership with suppliers. However, in practice nothing changed. Their buyers are still targeted on reducing costs and this means they shop around and force down our margins. If we point out the inconsistency between their leader's message and their behaviour — for if nothing else they are ignoring the costs of taking material from a variety of sources — they make it quite clear that if we raise these issues with people 'above' them, they'll drop us from the suppliers' list."

His point is that efficiencies can be gained by working together, not by the strong coercing the weak. But the American manufacturer's system can do no more than the latter. It has been designed that way. It was not the buyer's fault that he behaved that way, that's how he is measured — he is a product of his system.

Metal Co. sees the same amongst its British customers. The chief executive again:

> "Our British customers buy on price. If, for example, one has an order with us and then finds a cheaper source in the marketplace, typically they will ask us to hold their finished order as inventory. The same happens if they buy from us in bulk; they achieve a lower price but we or they then hold inventory. In a number of different ways they play suppliers off against each other."

This is the problem of attitude. It serves neither party to hold inventory. Neither is it simply an issue of cost. Many organisations embark on reduction of inventory to reduce cost. This is the wrong place to start, reflecting a traditional "command and control" view. When someone is "buying to budget", they will find it difficult to reduce the costs of the process. The paradox is that costs do fall as inventory falls, but the reduction of inventory is a consequence of working on flow. For example, achieving "batch sizes of one" or "single-piece flow" results in better quality and reduced waste.

Working to improve flow requires the methods associated with understanding the organisation as a system. Co-operation is a natural consequence of both parties following these methods. A system designed to improve quality would have roles designed to work between suppliers and customers (as the Japanese had), not roles designed to "optimise parts at the expense of the whole" (as the British and Americans had). Quality begins with a change in thinking.

To stay with Metal Co.'s sector:

> The chief executive of a "first-tier supplier" in the automotive sector had been proud to be the first to register to what was then BS 5750. His company was featured in a national newspaper in a major feature extolling the benefits of registration. We had kept a note of his name and by chance met with him some seven years later. He admitted that his company was like all others: that they had "done 5750" because they had to, that they rushed around to ensure that they would pass each audit and that it was a necessary condition of doing business in the UK. He also asserted that "clarifying procedures had been of benefit" but like others could not say how in any specific terms. When asked to feature in a national newspaper, he couldn't miss the opportunity it provided for publicity.

> When we met he was proudly saying that his company was aiming to be "amongst the first" to register to QS 9000. We asked him what the differences were between ISO 9000 and QS 9000. He did not know. We asked him what he knew about Taguchi's work and the theory of variation. He knew nothing. We asked why QS 9000 was important to him. "An opportunity for flag-waving," was his answer. "We were the first in our sector to get BS 5750, we want to be the first with this."

Deming used to say that quality is made in the boardroom. He was right.

LASER CO.

. . . thinking we've done quality when in reality we haven't even started

Background

"Laser Co." is a high-tech manufacturer, employing 150 people. Five years ago, a senior director (now the managing director) wanted greater discipline in the engineering function. Quality was chosen as a means. The quality manager wanted to introduce continuous improvement but needed a start and felt that ISO 9000 would provide the foundations.

The organisation has three main divisions: manufacturing, engineering and sales. Engineering had a history of high staff turnover and it was felt that the "wheel was continually being reinvented" — the organisation did not retain any semblance of "how we did it last time". A further influence was that larger customers were starting to "make noises" about the need for a quality system. They were beginning to feel obliged to respond lest they should find themselves unable to tender for business.

Laser Co. took advice from a consultant. They found his advice "dogmatic". It was also found to be misleading — for example, the consultant told them that traceability was a requirement of the Standard. They agonised over this for six months. Eventually, re-reading the Standard, they discovered that traceability was only important if the customer required it; theirs did not. They soon learned to work on their own interpretation of the Standard and not rely on the consultant. They knew, as they went into the exercise, that they wanted to avoid too much bureaucracy.

Implementation

Manufacturing found implementation to be very easy. The personnel in manufacturing were all used to working in a structured way: they used work tickets, time sheets and had a structured management information system (MRP). The focus in manufacturing was on writing down what they did. As this was happening the quality manager had to stop people in manufacturing from improving things — as they documented their procedures, people found obvious things to change. He was concerned that people should actually write down what they did (initially without instant modification). Having seen the more complete picture, he then encouraged review and improvements which were seized fairly eagerly. It is relevant to note the value that people got from clarifying their work procedures. Sometimes they were confronted with obvious things to change for the better. It makes one wonder what managers had been doing if they have not been doing that. Perhaps this shows how "attention to procedures" can be "bought" by managers as of palpable value and, hence, assumed to be "quality".

In engineering, implementation was more difficult. The prime purpose of introducing ISO 9000 into engineering was to establish a unified design process across the various groups. There was, prior to this, no defined method. Furthermore, the personnel in these groups were used to working in fairly ill-defined environments. To a large extent this meant starting implementation from scratch. They reviewed, for example, the engineering change process. People learned why the engineering change process had to be so involved — there were so many consequences stemming from engineering changes. With effort, implementation produced what was described as "remarkable" changes in engineering, mostly as a consequence of introducing procedures which would minimise the "reinventing of wheels".

Consistent with their desire to minimise bureaucracy, the implementation team dumped their procedures manuals in favour of flow charts. It kept the processes in focus in a simple and meaningful way; they had learned the value and importance of "clarity".

At the end of our discussion, the quality manager expressed the view that the whole process had one essential driver — the need to improve efficiency in an environment of economic recession and head count reductions. The whole effort took two-and-a-half years. Laser Co. claimed reductions in time, reduc-

tions in errors and reductions in waste. These were not quantified as no data were available. However, it is believable that
such gains might have been achieved. It was through the endeavours of two managers that this progress had been effected.
The two of them had to "make it happen". They felt it took a lot
of "getting through to people"; the MD's interest waned at times
(especially at end of quarter/year). Their view now, five years
on, is that ISO 9000 was the foundation for other things to happen. They felt that without it, they would have been unable to
get a company-wide focus for the quality effort.

Had ISO 9000 contributed to performance?

At the outset of this discussion, the efforts of the two people who
behaved as "organisational entrepreneurs" — working across
organisational barriers to make things happen — should be
recognised. It requires commitment and effort to create change
in organisations, usually due to fighting the current culture or
modus operandi. The managers argued that ISO 9000 registration produced benefits. Processes were more clearly defined,
resulting in less waste or more efficiency. They had recognised
and sought to avoid unnecessary bureaucracy, and even went a
further step away from the norm by getting rid of procedures,
using flow charts to provide clarity of focus.

Without doubt, this is a case where many of the usual excesses of ISO 9000 implementation had been avoided (excessive bureaucratisation and over-control through procedures).
Should that lead us to declare it a success? ISO 9000, if it is to
make a contribution, should improve economic performance,
both internally in how the company works and externally with
respect to the company's competitive position.

The extent to which ISO 9000 can or will improve economic
performance will depend on features of the Standard (and their
interpretation) and features of the company's current culture (or
management thinking). For this case, we will first consider the
impact of the current culture on performance.

This culture has various components, some of which we have
learned directly from the case study and some that we can assume from the clues we are given. Let us examine two:

Management by attention to output

During our discussion we learned that top management's attention "wavers from quality" at the end of financial periods. It is a sure sign that the company is run primarily on output data. It will follow that departments have budgets, targets, variance reporting (difference from target, etc.) and it then follows that time will be given over to discussion, defending, promoting and surviving the "budget issues". Management works this way when it has no understanding of the concepts of managing flow and variation. Enormous quantities of time are given over to irrelevant and stressful activity. The company does not benefit, it loses. The managers leading this implementation had continuous improvement as their long-term goal. Continuous improvement starts from an understanding of flow and variation — it is not an unending series of little "fixes" — and there was no end-to-end measurement in this system.

Work methods

Manufacturing found ISO 9000 straightforward because the methods were similar to the methods in use; it is normal in manufacturing to have work instructions, job sheets and so on. By contrast, what is normal in high-performance or world class systems? The Toyota Production System uses the following principles: single-piece flow, pull not push, control in the hands of operators (including the right to stop the line), and "automatic stops" on the line (if defective performance is detected).

While Laser Co. had cut time for internal processes, the total order fulfilment time had not changed and appeared to be inefficient when "value time" (the time used in making a product) was compared to "total time" (the time the product spent in their system). Lost time was probably only one type of waste being caused by the way work was designed and managed.

Management of flow is a fundamental principle of world class achievement. In Laser Co. the work methods were functionally designed and controlled and, by implication, there was no end-to-end management of flow.

Had ISO 9000 helped?

The ISO 9000 advocates would say that it had and in this case, as with some others, we might have been persuaded to agree. After all, the organisation has gained clarity, improved efficiency and avoided some "common pitfalls". Gaining clarity and improving efficiency are essentially the same gains sought by the founders of this movement in the bomb factories. The result, then as now, is the control of output. But quality is not only concerned with the control of output, it is concerned with improvement. Closer inspection of the way the organisation worked only raised doubts about ISO 9000's contribution to performance improvement.

What is most worrying is that the managers in this system might tell you that they have "done quality"; after all, they went through the steps as directed and achieved registration. How would this community respond if they were told there is an enormous amount still to do and it requires a fundamental rethink of current operating assumptions? This is a system which has no data about what matters to its customers, and is therefore unable to turn such data into useful measures. It shows no understanding of the importance and measurement of flow and variation. This is not a quality system, it is a "command and control" system. It is bound to be sub-optimised. The chances are they would rationalise the current position — after all, they have "got ISO 9000" — and hence any real opportunity for performance improvement would be lost.

This is a company that has avoided the worst of ISO 9000 and yet has been unable to avoid the fact that ISO 9000 registration has led it to a place from which it will be difficult to influence more fundamental change. ISO 9000 has reinforced some aspects of "business as usual", but it has not been the start of a quality journey. Even more disturbing is the fact that this process took two years. A company of only 150 people, if they learned to act on their organisation as a system, should be able to make changes to improve performance in months, not years. ISO 9000 has decreased the probability that change will be possible in this case. If this seemed a good case of ISO 9000 registration, we can only hope their competitors are as complacent.

LAN CO.

. . . the nightmare assessor

If Laser Co. would have been better served by knowing what mattered to its customers, "Lan Co." found out the hard way. Lan Co. is a network services company, providing its customers with networking solutions. In 1992, the owner decided he had to register to ISO 9000, as he did not want to be excluded from tenders. His customers were all government, health authorities, housing associations and large industrial companies. All were requiring their suppliers to have ISO 9000.

Lan Co. took advantage of the DTI scheme,[2] getting the services of a consultant at a subsidised price for 15 days. The consultant guided the owner, who had chosen to write the procedures himself. On each visit the consultant would outline how to approach each of the clauses and the owner would write the manual and associated documentation between visits. Having created the manual, procedures and work instructions, the owner brought in his installation crews to explain what ISO 9000 was about and what it meant for them. This was the first sign of trouble. Installation crews did not see the value of having to sign "as seen and understood" changes to work instructions; they were resistant to what they saw to be an affront to their common sense. Nevertheless, all installers were trained and the associated training records completed.

As it was a business that involved design, Lan Co. had become registered to ISO 9001. The owner remarked that it was not always perceived as an advantage. His friends told him that other companies were further ahead than him because they had ISO 9002! In fact ISO 9001 has more requirements than ISO 9002 in that it includes design control. But the real disadvantage of registration was to rear its head very quickly. The owner explained:

---

[2] A UK government scheme designed to share the costs of registration to ISO 9000.

"Design control became a major problem. We couldn't find a satisfactory way to suit our customers and suit the assessor. The Standard works fine if you go to site, prepare a set of drawings, agree what is to be done for the client and then nothing changes. But things do change, it is the nature of the business we are in. In many cases the clients change their mind, they make minor changes to equipment siting or requirements. Of course we respond — after all, we are a service business, but the trouble it caused with the assessor was unbelievable."

We asked how many contracts were subject to change after acceptance — the answer was around 30 per cent. To continue:

"ISO 9000 required any change to be recorded. In simple terms this meant re-drawing or adding amendments to the specification and going through the process of agreeing the same with the customer. With large contracts that was fine but with small contracts it was totally inefficient."

We asked how many of each the business had in a year. His answer was about five large contracts, worth about 40 per cent of total revenue, and about 200 smaller contracts which accounted for about 60 per cent of revenue. The problem he had was that the assessors would specifically look for changes to the contract. He was unable to fulfil the requirements of the Standard as required by his assessors and remain in business, so he devised a work-around: Every job had a design control form (according to the guidance of the assessor); if a change was required by the customer it was recorded on the design control document and the "all aspects clear" box ticked. The box was ticked regardless of whether the changes had been translated into additional drawings and signed as accepted by the customer, but now the owner was at risk of being caught out by his assessor.

The owner justified this course of action to himself:

"We are a service business. It is normal for customers to change their minds. Sometimes they want extra terminals, sometimes they want to change the location of PCs. Whatever they want is what we are there to provide. Most of these jobs were for hundreds of pounds, few were for more than two thousand pounds. The customers would expect us to listen to their needs and respond. They didn't value the design control procedure any more than we did. ISO 9000 was creating a monster which was serving no one's needs except the assessor's. I would despair. One of our major customers was a health authority and I would say to myself we are not supplying a battleship. I was not being paid by the authority for design changes and neither did it matter to the people whose PCs we were connecting that we did not stop work and rewrite our work orders every time they changed their minds. In fact it was positively getting in the way of good relationships when we did. They were in a constant state of change. They wanted us to respond to their needs.

The assessor was keen to make hay on this issue. On one occasion during a customer site visit he cited the lack of customer verification of changes to an order as a non-conformance. The installation crews concerned knew that the customer didn't want to be hassled and there was no evidence of customers being in dispute or withholding payment because of contractual problems. But it was a problem for the assessor."

Lan Co. wanted to look after its customers' needs, but registration to ISO 9000 meant satisfying assessors over and above satisfying customers. Inevitably, Lan Co. learned that the only solution was to fiddle the paperwork to avoid hassle with the assessor.

"Assessment visits were always argumentative, it was as though their job was to catch you doing something wrong. The major fights were always over documentation. For example, if we changed a work procedure and failed to register that change in document control we were in for a 'right going over'. The slightest change to a procedure involved us in hours of work. If you changed a procedure you had to change the quality manual. In turn, these changes had to be recorded in document control. Then the new procedure had to be published and the people who would use that procedure in their work had to be informed. This required getting them together and having them sign a piece of paper to confirm that they had knowledge of the changes and then that had to be recorded as having happened. Such changes then required the recall and amendment of all of the quality manuals.

I found myself being tied to the office. The assessors assured me that if I got the management system working properly it would ensure that the organisation turned out a quality performance. It was a nightmare. I found myself becoming more and more detached from the business, knowing less and less about customers as I became embroiled in the paperwork created by ISO 9000. It was a method of management whose focus was procedures, documentation and control; it was not about customers and the people who provided service to them. For two years I stood in front of my staff telling them that this made sense, was necessary and was the same as everybody else was doing. But you can't ignore the obvious futility forever and the longer you do, the less your staff respect you.

In the days before ISO 9000, when a change was made to the way the organisation worked people were told about it. There were often changes because of the nature of the work; changes to software and hardware standards were frequent in a fast-moving area of technology. The culture of the organisation had changed from 'telling people', to 'telling people, writing about it, getting them to sign to indicate they had been told and then writing about that'. We knew this was silly, but it became a case of doing what had to be done to secure the contracts we were seeking.

I would dread the assessors coming in. They would claim they were interested in continuous improvement. They would go through the paperwork and check for details. For example, design control forms were numbered. There were five people in the company who did quotes and they would give their work to a secretary for word processing. It was her job to type a draft and return it for final editing. When it was completed she would attach a design control form and give the job a number. All quotes would then go to my desk for final signature."

Who felt responsible? If the originator felt that the secretary would "sort out" any missing bits and she felt that others would, because they create them or sign them, it would introduce errors. Whenever more than one person is responsible, you get an increase in errors.

> "From time to time the secretary would miss a number in the series. It would attract the attention of the assessor. He would want to know whether this was a job and was missing its paperwork or whether the secretary had made an error. In either case the assessor would record a non-conformance and would expect to see evidence of corrective action on his next visit. Typically, I had to write about what I had done to prevent reoccurrence, for example, conducting further training of the secretary."

Of course this was not a training problem — the assessor showed a failure to distinguish between common-cause and special-cause. Moreover, the errors were being caused by the way the work was designed and managed and the assessors had been the architects.

> "To avoid getting into grief with the assessor, I'd document non-conformances I'd spotted which I couldn't correct in time — and almost all of these related to customer contract issues — so that if the assessor spotted them I could show that a non-conformance report was already in the system. It became a game preventing them catching us doing something 'wrong'."

His antipathy to the assessor only grew:

> "Our assessors were to assess us for on-site accreditation. On our first assessment the assessors were unable to assess on-site work because they had not yet achieved the required registration as an assessing body. It made me furious. Here was a company assessing mine which was not itself accredited with the competence to do the work. The consultants were quite relaxed about what I thought was a glaring discrepancy. I could only recall all the pain they had put me through on matters of contract review and felt

conned that they didn't have to pay the same regard to their dealings with clients."

We asked what he thought "continuous improvement" meant to the assessors:

"Their attitude disappointed me. They never took an interest in what we did. For them 'continuous improvement' meant paperwork. They would go ever deeper into different parts of the business, I felt that they wanted to 'bash every area'. After each visit from the assessors we would have what we described as 'homework' — paperwork to do to correct the paper system. Things required changing, cross-referencing and updating. The assessors were inconsistent. Each would take a slightly different view of what was important. Sometimes we would find ourselves telling an assessor that what he was asking us to do would overturn what his more senior colleague had instructed us to set up."

He learned how to deal with assessors:

"We used to cheat. We'd put things in the ladies toilet, safe in the knowledge that no assessor could find them (all assessors were male): spare parts which had come back from jobs, which the assessors would expect to be labelled; scraps of paper which staff might have used to work out a quote — the assessors would pick up such scraps and argue that the work was at risk of being lost and that there ought to be a form on which calculations were made; customer drawings which did not have numbers; all of these things would be hidden away to avoid grief. I'd get as many staff out of the office as possible: if the assessors couldn't ask them questions, they'd be less able to find things to criticise. The assessors view was 'You have to decide whether or not you want it' (ISO 9000). Their attitude was condescending. We put our procedures onto a computer. Immediately the assessor criticised us for allowing all staff to have access. They insisted that we create a password protection and we were obliged to give a copy of the password to one of the assessors who told us that he lodged it with their firm's accountant along with an instruction to open it only upon his death. It was like being in the secret service."

And what did ISO 9000 cost him?

> "ISO 9000 registration cost us £50,000 in the first eighteen
> months, from start to first registration. I feel like it's the only
> time I have paid money to have a hard time. With the same
> money I could have invested in technical equipment and
> improved the service we offered to our customers."

But despite it all he had not given up on quality:

> "We did a survey of our customers, asking them what mat-
> tered to them and how they found our services. What we
> learned was that ISO 9000 registration was irrelevant to the
> people who used our services. We learned that it was the
> purchasing departments who were demanding ISO 9000
> registration of suppliers. We found that our customers were
> getting irritated with 'being chased for signatures' —
> something which was only occurring because of ISO 9000."

Clearly ISO 9000 was making matters worse.

The owner of Lan Co. had other views of his experience with
assessors:

> "The assessors wanted installation engineers to carry their
> procedures manuals and up-to-date network standards in-
> formation. The latter were very expensive, it would have
> been economically impossible to maintain. Management
> review was a farce. Having had a discussion about what we
> were doing, we would find ourselves having to say, 'You
> know what we just talked about? Well now we're going to
> write the same and sign it.' It was like saying that people
> don't have brains and can't be trusted. One positive ad-
> vantage was that you could always find the paperwork asso-
> ciated with a job if and when it was needed in the future.
> Not a high-frequency occurrence, but valuable neverthe-
> less."

Some benefit in comparison to the sub-optimisation he was experiencing. The assessors had forced a production view of the
world on him. He needed something to help him develop his
service view.

SYSTEMS CO.

. . . is ISO 9000 a good starting place?

"Systems Co." is an engineering services organisation which manufactures handling systems and installs the same on customer sites. The customers use the systems in their manufacturing and packaging operations. Systems Co. has been registered to ISO 9000 for a number of years. To achieve initial registration, Systems Co. sought the help of an accredited assessment body. Having interviewed several, they chose one which they felt demonstrated the least "bureaucratic" attitude and showed the most desire to be helpful and constructive in the relationship.

In this case, we followed a routine surveillance inspection being conducted by the firm of outside assessors. As the assessor worked we kept an interest in two questions: what is he looking for and why? The second question leads to a corollary: does this help improve the system? The assumption was that this would tell us about what the assessor (and client) thought about the Standard and how their thinking related to quality issues in the organisation.

Prior to our meeting, the client informed us that the assessor was "one of the better ones". We took this to mean that he would take a view of the organisation as a business system rather than be pedantic about (his) interpretation of the Standard. We had been told that the assessor's organisation had "recognised that their market has shifted to a focus on things that had benefit to the business". The client saw the inspection process as one of "support and assistance" to the business.

In this routine surveillance (described as a "health check"), the assessor focused on several "mandatory" issues and then selected three areas of the business. The purpose of the inspection was to raise any items of non-conformance which, if found, would be given an agreed date for resolution.

The mandatory issues were:

- **Changes to personnel**. We probed why. We were told that change to a significant position (for example, the chief executive) would require investigation as to whether this could adversely impact the quality system. The criteria for choosing whether to investigate such changes were specified in a manual produced by the assessing organisation's quality system.

To summarise the discussion that ensued: If the chief executive were to change, how could an inspection determine whether to record what he sees as a non-conformance? The assessor would seek evidence of the new leader's commitment to the quality system through words and deeds. It seems to us that this is a method that relies on anecdote and interpretation. What chief executive would not assert that he or she was "up for quality"? Would chairing quality reviews be sufficient to be evidence that he or she was doing things in support of the quality system? A judgement must be made; yet any decision could only be based on the assessor's view of the world.

- **Changes to equipment**. This follows the same logic as the above to the extent that the assessor takes a view on what equipment changes should be subject to review.

- **Changes to the documented management system**. Any changes should be reviewed to ensure they are consistent with the requirements of the Standard. Once again, decisions are based on the assessor's view of his own quality system, the client's quality system and, above all, his interpretation of the Standard.

- **Results and corrective actions from internal audits**. It is relevant to note that at the time of first registration the client had established a group of internal inspectors (according to advice from the original consultants). The group has since been disbanded. When the chief executive was appointed he charged the quality manager with changing the way quality was working away from "quality control" and towards prevention and improvement. He took the view that control should be in the hands of people doing the work. The chief executive also charged the quality manager with

reducing the documented quality system from two manuals
to 15 pages.

- **Feedback from customers**. Complaints, returns and any
  corrective actions. Again, this relies on the assessor's interpretation (for example, whether problems should be treated
  as "special-cause" or "common-cause").

- **Management review**. To stand back and determine the effectiveness of the quality system. Again, this is subject to
  interpretation by the assessor — what might be the assessor's mental model of the purpose and mechanics of the
  management review?

- **Use of the assessor's logo**. Apparently, the assessing organisation was implementing a directive from the UK Accreditation Service that dictated requirements for the proper
  use of "quality badges" on stationery and the like. In this
  case the issue was irrelevant, the chief executive had already decided that he saw no value in "advertising for the
  assessor".

The three areas of the business the assessor inspected in detail
were engineering, manufacturing and customer service.

Engineering

In engineering, the assessor inspected a customer file. This file
records customer information. The assessor was interested in
how the system made sure the customer got what was expected: how drawings were numbered, how people would
know they were working on the right drawing, that the right information went to the right places, and how, if changes were
made, they were accommodated.

The assessor followed the progress of a file through to
manufacturing. He was interested in how the jobs "came in",
how the system tracked changes, and how work was planned
through the manufacturing resources.

This is "bomb factory" quality — adherence to procedures.
It seems plausible that work should be tidy, orderly and accurate. It is "just in case" thinking. It does have merit and can, in

some circumstances, be of value but it is essentially a means of control, not improvement. In bomb factories it dealt with the immediate problem, it controlled output. It is indeed plausible, even reasonable, to presume that the control of drawings, changes and relevant customer information will help ensure that the customer gets what the customer wants. It clearly could affect quality if these things went wrong and were not repaired before something reached the customer. But if we are controlling these things it should be because we have *demonstrated* their influence over the quality of output, not on the basis of "just in case". We should instead question whether the right things are being controlled.

Why did the organisation develop this "control of activity" approach to quality? Because they had learned it from their consultants and assessors. Even though they are cutting back on it, it is still the principle means of quality control — and all it can do is control output. It should be termed management control, not quality control.

Quality is concerned with improvement. Improvement requires action on the system. In this case the only action on the system encouraged by the introduction of ISO 9000 was inspecting for non-conformance and the management review. The system was assumed to be in control if people behaved according to procedures. However, these procedures do not necessarily relate to what matters to customers, and subsequently may or may not tell us more about the performance of a process.

It is fundamental to quality thinking that measures (and controls) should be related to purpose. What is the purpose of this system? If it is to be a quality organisation, the measures in use should tell us how well it works and whether things are improving. This system had no data concerning what mattered to customers. There were customer surveys, but the items were written internally so it was impossible to determine if they understood what mattered to their customers. If they had known, they might have been able to turn "what mattered" into internal operational measures to track action for improvement. To take two possible examples: how often do they deliver assembled product on time as originally committed? There were no data readily available, although everybody estimated 75 per cent. How often can the engineers complete their work on-site without recourse to manufacturing for something that should have been foreseen? There were no data; estimates ranged from hardly ever to nearly always.

Manufacturing

In manufacturing the manager used measures of labour hours. The purpose was to charge hours to jobs. It is not an unusual measure: many organisations do this. The assumption is that improving utilisation of the labour force will improve efficiency, hence lowering costs. The manager's task is to ensure that jobs keep to budget. This is the classic problem of "budget management": the starting number is a reasonable guess from the contracting department, and any variation between the starting number and the final number could be due to a variety of causes. Minor variations are ignored, major variations are reported although there is no evidence of whether these are common-cause or special-cause and, in any event, the starting number was a "guess". If major variations are acted upon, what can the manager do? The likelihood is that any action will result in distortion of the system, the priority being to "be seen to come in on budget", so the manager might shift labour around to suit budgets, not customers. The managers told us that "no distortion of data or other dishonest actions occurred here" and that may be so. The point is it's more likely that they will. More importantly, this is the type of data which could be dangerous if used to drive a "get costs down" understanding of improvement.

Improvement starts with understanding what matters to customers and then improving the flow of work. The data which might help learning and improvement (thus reducing costs down *and* improving service) was not in use: how predictable is our delivery versus first commitment? How often are engineers able to fit the customers' equipment without returning for something which should have been catered for? What are the type and frequency of customer and engineer demands on the organisation?

In this, the manufacturing side of the organisation, the prevailing attitudes were more in tune with the implicit attitude of the Standard. People placed a high value on having the correct procedures and the right documentation ("doing things right" rather than "doing the right thing"). When we discussed some of the features of the system which, if understood, might lead to improvement, the general response reflected an assumption that these things were normal. But there were no data, and no methods for improvement.

Customer service

Customer service was the assessor's final area to inspect and it is fair to say that he said something that surprised us. He was interested in:

- Whether the organisation had determined how often to conduct customer surveys

- How the results of such surveys were being built back into the management system

- How the organisation knew what mattered to its customers.

It was the last item that surprised us. Having seen so many organisations (including this one) dwelling on control of the customer's order and because of the emphasis placed on this by the "contract review" clause of the Standard, it was a nice surprise to hear an assessor emphasise that "what mattered to the customer" mattered.

However, the assessor was primarily concerned to relate customer survey data to the management system. He assumed that "what mattered to customers" was being measured by the customer satisfaction survey. Indeed, it is typical of many organisations that vast quantities of customer satisfaction surveys are used, but with little understanding of what matters. His line of thought was concerned with "corrective" actions as defined by the management system (as written) and their reporting. The chief executive preferred to see the data as something which would drive action in the relevant part of the business, without a formal management decision structure over it (he subscribes to the view that action is of more value than reports). This approach was characteristic of the changes the chief executive had made to the way the organisation worked.

It would have been of greater value to the organisation if the assessor had focused on the methods employed to gather customer data and the development and use of related measures to improve performance. For example, interviews with customers showed that they wanted quotations when they requested them (not within a period). The contracting department took immediate action by controlling this with the use of a white-board: customers' desired dates for quotations were written up for all to see, which improved performance immediately — they had acted on what mattered to their customers. The use of a white-board would make this procedure "difficult" to inspect — in our experience many assessors like to inspect documents and are not comfortable assessing notes on white-boards and the like.

The contracting department also learned that 75 per cent of all quotations work resulted in no order. It was a healthy perspective to take, the sort of view a systems-thinker would take — they were using a measure related to purpose. The department had started doing work on understanding the causes, but this work had, so far, not included data from customers. But it was typical of the way things were working in the more progressive parts of the organisation — people had the right (systems) perspective and only needed help with method.

When we asked how people were measured in the contracting department, we were told there were no individual performance measures. We regarded this as a good response. Typically in such departments one finds "activity measures" used in such a way as to undermine performance. The measures in use in contracting related to purpose (quotation on-time as committed, revenue); the use of these will be more likely to contribute to a climate of improvement. In other parts of the organisation, more traditional attitudes prevailed. It is not to suggest that people differed in their commitment and potential contribution. Our experience has taught us just how much be- haviour is conditioned by features of the organisation which we call system conditions, and measurement is a very influential system condition.

Had ISO 9000 been beneficial?

The quality manager claimed so. He argued (as do others) that ISO 9000 was a good starting place for the quality journey.

There is no doubt that clarity is an aid to good performance. But if with clarity comes unnecessary documentation and inappropriate controls, has it been beneficial? This organisation has spent the last three years drawing back from and eradicating dysfunctional aspects of registration to ISO 9000. Should this be regarded as a necessary cost? Surely not. It was argued that ISO 9000 gave the organisation the impetus. Wouldn't it have been more beneficial to allow the customers to be the impetus? If so, wouldn't the organisation have moved more quickly along the road of discovering the right methods and measures to improve performance?

Systems Co. is an organisation which is learning to behave as a "customer-driven system". Yet was this learning facilitated or hindered by registration to ISO 9000? It could only have been hindered. ISO 9000 registration had focused on documentation of, and adherence to, procedures. There was no evidence (other than anecdotal) as to the consequences on performance and plenty of evidence of the scope for performance improvement.

UTILITY CO.

. . . standards mean worse service

Privatisation of utility companies has been accompanied by their regulation: monopoly suppliers must be controlled against abusing their position. The regulators are people of their time; they seek to impose conditions or constraints on the regulated, and to do so they employ thinking which is current and to them, no doubt, plausible. As we shall see, this has resulted in the accommodation of ISO 9000 as a preferred means of control, and it is having a destructive affect on the performance of utility companies.

The Electricity Regulator has published "Best Practice Standards". The regulator is concerned to ensure that information about customer service standards is reliable and consistent over time and between companies. It seems a reasonable thing to establish and it suggests that we will be able to learn and improve. In giving regional electricity companies (RECs) guidance about how to achieve this aim, the Regulator states: "The requirements are similar to those specified in ISO 9000." The regulator implies that if an REC has ISO 9000, it will meet the requirements of "best practice".

The Regulator expects RECs to establish and publish service standards, and then to report breaches of these standards in such a way as to allow inspections and reviews to be conducted. The procedures must cover how "breaches" are identified, recorded, reviewed and reported. The reporting system must include structure charts, job descriptions, training records and a defined process for reporting. This whole effort should have an appointed representative and should be documented. The levels of documentation required are specified and changes or any document control should also be defined and documented. All "failures to conform" to the documented system have to be recorded and subject to corrective action and, finally, the whole system should be subjected to internal and external inspections. It is easy to see how the Regulator thinks that ISO 9000 will cover all of the requirements.

What happens in practice? Firstly, the RECs produce service standards and send them to their customers. It seems to us that very few people will read these leaflets; none of us has and when we ask others we find few who have and those few usually cannot remember the contents. The standards are entirely arbitrary, they are not set with an understanding of the REC's capability. Some examples of our own REC's guarantees:

> "If your main fuse fails, we will arrive within four hours of your call. If we take longer, we will give you 20 pounds."

> If your supply fails due to a problem with our system, we will restore it within 24 hours of first becoming aware of the situation (excepting exceptional circumstances). If we don't succeed and you let us know within a month, we'll give you 40 pounds (100 pounds for business customers).
>
> If you are concerned about your meter, we will reply to you within five working days or visit your home within ten working days. If we take longer we will pay you 20 pounds."

And so on they go. It seems to us that customers don't want guarantees, they want service. They don't want recompense, they want action. As we shall see, the action caused by these standards is undermining performance. Some examples:

> One regional electricity company (REC) has set up a method to avoid failing on guarantees for appointments; if they know they are going to fail to meet a guarantee, they phone the customer to re-arrange the appointment. In this way it is not recorded and reported as a failure.

This is normal behaviour when people are subject to arbitrary controls.[3] The ingenuity of people becomes engaged in fighting the system. It results in distortion, demoralisation and, hence, sub-optimisation:

> If the person who made the appointment is not the customer as defined by the name on the bill (for example, wife, husband, son, daughter, neighbour, etc.), any failure to keep an appointment is not regarded as a failure because the commitment was not made to the "lawful" customer.

The contractual thinking implicit in ISO 9000 is given full rein, as is the thinking about procedures and people:

> Failures to meet service standards are recorded on a form which requires the name of the "person responsible". Failure forms create fear. They also ask "what action was taken by the manager in respect of the person responsible?"

---

[3] See *I Want You to Cheat*, Seddon, Vanguard Press, 1992.

It is assumed that all failures should result in action to prevent re-occurrence; a failure to understand the distinction between special cause and common cause variation. Action on every failure will inevitably lead to increasing variation and less control; it will make performance worse.

Managers of these organisations are heard to say "heads will roll" if there is a failure on service guarantees; as a result, their staff become preoccupied with covering up failure. The consequence is that the only thing that can be guaranteed is that the Regulator will get unreliable data. Perhaps their response, as they discover this, will be to tighten controls. If it is, it will be evidence that they are not learning either. The Regulator is afflicted by the same thinking as the ISO 9000 fraternity. To believe that work should be defined, controlled, documented and audited is to make work less efficient and less attractive to customers.

> A repair crew arrived at a customer's house late in the evening. The customer's supply was down and the crew were about to dig up the garden. The customer would have been happy for the crew to start in the morning but to do so would have been to fail to meet their service standard. The crew did as they should (to meet the need of the customer) and misreported the incident to avoid attention from their managers.

When a customer telephones or writes to their REC, they want a response to the problem, not an acknowledgement in a specified number of days. Customers are less interested in filling in forms to get recompense than seeing their REC work on improving the quality of service delivered. The "standards system" is not capable of being used for improvement and will cause a rise in complaints and bad "word of mouth". The measures required for improvement lie elsewhere.

Service standards are assumed to make service better. The Government Minister for the Citizen's Charter put it this way:

> "The way to improve service is to set a standard, publish performance and give people the means to complain when performance is not to standard."

He could not be more wrong. When you set a standard (with no understanding of what current performance is predictably achieving) a host of problems occur. When the standard is below current performance, people slow down, they work "to the standard". When the standard is unachievable in terms of current performance, people do whatever they can to avoid being caught or "failing". There are many examples of these phenomena occurring throughout public and private sector organisations. People are not learning about and improving their work, they are doing whatever it takes to avoid remonstration.

One consequence is that published data are always unreliable or "distorted". League tables do not motivate or teach, they only de-motivate. "Standards" thinking also adds to costs — now we have bureaucracies of standards-setters, procedures writers, internal and external auditors and complaint handlers. Complaints are rising. We could have spent the same money solving the problems.

If, for example, the RECs knew more about the predictability of customer demand on their system and the predictability of their current response, they would be in a position to start work on improvement. We will explore how these simple ideas would have resulted in a far better solution for these and other organisations in our next chapter.

What can we learn from the case studies?

Any of these cases — and every other case of ISO 9000 registration we have researched — could have made great strides in improving quality and performance, and could have done so in a much shorter time than was devoted to ISO 9000. Some were more grossly off the point than others. To see their opportunities for improvement the managers of these organisations would have needed to take a different view, a view which the ISO 9000 experience had prevented them seeing. Worse still, ISO 9000 registration led many of these managers to assume they had "done quality" (or service) when, as we have said before, nothing could be further from the truth.

The cases are not exciting examples of positive change. Despite seeking them for the last five years, we have yet to find *any* exciting changes associated with ISO 9000. There is nothing to enthuse about and plenty to question. Not only was little achieved in those which might be argued to be the best cases of ISO 9000 registration, but some have clearly taken a step backwards. We have also seen how registration to ISO 9000 involved considerable time and resources — resources which might have been employed in a better way.

Are these cases unusual or unrepresentative? Not in our experience. In April 2000, in conjunction with Takaji Nisizawa, a leading industrial consultant in Japan, we undertook a further round of case studies.

Takaji Nishizawa asked us to arrange visits with small to medium size organisations in the manufacturing sector. The six organisations visited comprised two automotive suppliers, both of which were registered to QS 9000, a metal box manufacturer, a label maker, a paint maker and a specialist supplier of measurement equipment.

Takaji Nishizawa was concerned to learn how these organisations had interpreted ISO 9000 in practice. Between visits we discussed the organisations' general approach to management and whether or not they were improving performance. In short, those that were improving were doing so in spite of the Standard — they had avoided letting the Standard impede their operations. That is the best that can be said for ISO 9000 registration. It can impede operational performance and implementation should be managed closely to ensure it does not.

Four themes emerged from these visits:

Bureaucracy versus simplicity

The best example of a quality manual was the label maker. They had integrated the quality manual and management procedures. Each part of the manual began with a high-level flow of the end-to-end process. Each subsequent procedure followed the hierarchical format of purpose, measures and method — where the measures in use related to the purpose of the process and method was a flow diagram of the process. Similarly, the metal box manufacturer organisation had integrated the quality manual and management procedures, reducing the documentation to a minimum. The specialist supplier of measurement equipment was working towards a simpler and combined quality manual, but at the time of our visit, the quality manual was some 350 pages long.

By contrast, the two automotive suppliers that were registered to QS 9000 had enormous volumes of paperwork and the associated bureaucracy (form-filling, etc) extended to the work areas. To take one example of the bureaucracy: Consistent with the requirements of the Standard, the automotive suppliers had corrective action procedures. In one, Takaji Nishizawa asked: "How many non-conformances have been reported?" The answer was five by customers and two internally over the last year. Takaji Nishizawa knew immediately this was not a good system. Given the volume of goods being manufactured there were too few problems. It is not unusual to find bureaucracy stifling intent — to declare a non-conformance is to risk trouble. It ought to be a source of learning. But for that to be the case, the way people behave has to change (see below).

The paint maker, which was registered to ISO 9001, also had an enormous number of quality manuals, written to satisfy the assessor's requirements for each business unit to have its own manuals. Interestingly, the work flow in the paint maker was very simple, they mixed and canned paints. The working areas were not clean, there was abundant inventory, some of which was clearly old and, most important of all, the organisation appeared not to be learning. The bulk of non-conformances reported were for colour matching. The data appeared to be stable over time (although they were not used to establish capability — what the system was predictably achieving), in other words, this system can be expected to have such problems unless something is changed. Aside from the scope for improving the measurement and control of raw materials, Takaji Nishizawa saw a further probable cause of failure. He asked if this organisation specified the method of application — how the paint should be used by the customer. The answer was no.

Use and misuse of quality tools

Takaji Nishizawa was concerned that some of these organisations had employed quality tools but without understanding them, hence the tools were of no value. For example, in two cases they had "tried" Kanban in conditions for which it was not appropriate. In the first, the line was not a flow; hence Kanban would not improve anything. In the second, the line was making to stock, so the benefits of Kanban would not be realised.

The approach to error–cause–removal in the automotive manufacturers was bureaucratic and unlikely to lead to learning. In keeping with the requirements of the Standard, non-conformances were identified by declared means (for example, SPC alert and corrective action reporting). The non-conformances were then reported and subject to later analysis. Takaji Nisizawa was concerned that this approach would lead to loss of knowledge. To use his expression, "the truth has gone". He maintains that the right way to learn is to attend the non-conformance when and where it happens — this is why the operatives on the Toyota line can and do stop the line. If a non-conformance is studied at source, no data is lost — the data tell the truth, they will not be turned into a representation of the truth. Then a hypothesis can be formed and tested. In that way, learning occurs.

In a further example of incorrect use of tools, one organisation employed "visual control" — displays at the work stations describing what "good work" looked like. However, these displays were complex and had, as Takaji Nishizawa observed, "much small writing" — they were unlikely to be useable by the operatives who, in any event, kept their heads down throughout the period of observation. It was, he observed, as thought they were there for the sake of being there, not for the purpose of helping the operatives do better work. Takaji Nishizawa made the following observation:

> "These managers are confusing two types of information. Information that is common and should be known by all is to be used for training and should not be needed as visual control. Information that is specific (to a customer's job) is needed for visual control and should be available to the op-

erator. When managers fail to make this distinction confusion arises."

To make everything available, as was the case here, runs the risk of employees feeling they are being taught to suck eggs — a sure cause of demoralisation.

Design control versus process control

Takaji Nishizawa made a profound observation on the implicit theory of the Standard. He noted that the Standard treats design control and process control as separate clauses. In fact, it does not raise the subject of process design at all, leaving process management to be thought of in procedural terms. To quote Takaji Nishizawa:

> "Quality is made in the process. You cannot, or should not, separate product design from process design as the Standard does.[4] Process design builds quality in and waste out as has been shown in the Toyota production system and in using Taguchi's methods. The Standard focuses managers on the control of product or service design and, separately, takes a 'procedures' approach to processes — there is insufficient attention to process methods — how quality will be made."

Takaji Nishizawa used the following simple diagram to illustrate his point:

Figure 6.1 Design and Process Should be Thought of as Integrated

---

[4] The revised Standard maintains the separation of product and process design.

Leadership

Of the six organisations we visited, three showed evidence of genuine and sustainable improvements in their operations. However, this had nothing to do with ISO 9000 and everything to do with their leaders. All three leaders had undergone personal learning experiences. One had travelled with a Japanese *sensei* (expert) while the expert went around the organisation's sites in America. One had taken a trip to Japan to study with a *sensei*. The third was already down the road of systems thinking and was very concerned to take a systems approach to ISO 9000 registration and hence avoid the usual bureaucracy and suboptimisation associated with the more usual application.

But the impact of the leaders went beyond this. Two described their experiences with quality managers and ISO 9000 assessors. To quote one:

> "In every meeting with the assessor, I argued for what was right for my business and I would not be influenced to do things that did not help. I also fired three quality managers for spending too much time working with quality documentation from their offices and not on the shop floor, where quality is made. This behaviour made them more susceptible to being influenced by the assessors. In my experience the assessors are not up to the job. They don't get paid enough, so the general standard is low. They generally lack knowledge — they focus on the Standard and are afraid to look at processes. Many have old-fashioned ideas; they have little understanding of how to manage a business. For that reason I kept all of our improvement work outside of the documented quality system, because I did not want the assessor interfering with something he would not understand."

The other did likewise. He kept the quality manual deliberately vague. He said:

> "I don't want it to be precise, that would give the assessor more things to pick on. If the specifics are there the assessors will focus on them. We were concerned to ensure that ISO 9000 would only be looked at from the point of view of

how it might add value to the business, nothing else mattered. We integrated our management procedures within the quality manual, which is only ten pages long, and kept them to a minimum. For example, we have no self-generated work instructions, the work instructions are the customers' drawings; our people use their brains and decide in each case how best to make them."

In summary, Takaji Nishizawa sought to learn whether the same problems were occurring in both Japan and the UK and how people were dealing with such problems. He found that the same problems were occurring and he was particularly concerned about the problems caused by the poor quality of assessors. The solution was for managers to take responsibility and lead rather than follow their assessors. For managers to lead in a productive way, it would help them significantly to know about the principles and practice of managing flow — the secret behind the Toyota Production System. This is a prerequisite to the appropriate use of tools.

Takaji Nishizawa has developed a nine-point plan for organisations that want to get the best out of ISO 9000 implementation. This is reproduced with his permission as an Appendix.

The prerequisite for managing flow is to understand the organisation as a system. This is what visitors to Japan did not "see" during the 1970s. It is central to understanding the better way.

Chapter 7

THERE IS A BETTER WAY

The better way begins with understanding the organisation as a system. When working with managers who are leading change in their organisations, we have found it important to help them make distinctions between "command and control" thinking and "systems" thinking.

Managers have been conditioned to believe that the job of management (decision-making) is separated from work. Following the ideas of Alfred Sloan we have built "budget-responsible" hierarchical organisations; the managers who work in them do what is expected of them. To manage their organisation as a system, managers need to learn what to do differently and what to stop doing. In simple terms, systems thinking reconnects management with work — it is a better way to make the work work.

In this chapter we reconsider what was learned from the case studies and discuss what they might have done if the managers had been shown a better way. To remind you of the distinctions between the two ways of thinking, we reproduce them here (Figure 7.1).

A better perspective

"Make and sell" is a fundamental tradition in "command and control" management thinking. It is to think "push" rather than "pull". Factories build products, marketing and sales sell them. There are always arguments concerning whether and how well the decisions about what is produced are based on customer needs. "Pull" thinking, on the other hand, assumes it is better to make to order; to ensure the customer "pulls" value from the system. It cuts time, inventory and waste; "pull" results in improved quality. When you discuss these ideas with traditional "make and sell" managers they are initially resistant. After all, they are preoccupied with production costs and they fail to see how costs will fall is the factory only makes what is demanded.

Figure 7.1 Command and Control versus Systems Thinking

	Command and Control Thinking	**Systems Thinking**
Perspective	Top-down hierarchy, functional procedures	Outside-in, process and "flow"
Attitude to Customers	Contractual	What matters?
Decision-making	Separated from work	Integrated with work
Measurement	Output, targets, standards: related to budget	Capability, variation: related to purpose
Attitude to Suppliers	Contractual	Co-operative
Ethos	Control	Learning

Laser Co. was an example of the traditional manufacturing attitude. They could have made great strides by changing to a "pull" system. ISO 9000 serves to maintain a "make" or "push" view because of its antecedents in the new and technological manufacturing sectors. The Standard asks managers to think in terms of how procedures control production. A better question would be *"how does the system manage demand and flow?"* Systems Co. was closer to "pull" thinking: they assembled to order. But the organisation still showed a traditional manufacturing attitude in the management of the core processes: they had no measures which related to how well they responded to demand — the first step in managing flow. All the measures in use related to costs.

Attention to costs sub-optimises performance. Managers become concerned with "making their numbers" at the expense of the system. The real costs are in the system — delays, duplication, errors, time, materials and so on — and most of these don't show up on management accounts. Management accounts do have limited value. They tell you what has happened, but they don't tell you what is *going* to happen. It might be logical to assume that if every function makes its budget, the organisation is performing well. But if managers are using budgetary measures to manage, they will be ignorant of the causes of costs and will often take action that makes things worse.

"Management by the numbers" is the ethos of management's traditional role. It translates into "define and do" — towards all features of work. In Tech Co. we saw how procedures became more important than purpose. Not only did this make things worse for the customer, it also damaged morale. In Metal Co. we saw how following the rules (procedures) slowed down work. Laser Co. illustrated how the logic of procedures fits with a traditional view of manufacturing. Here is another example:

> We studied a lift factory which was registered to ISO 9000. We found it was spending half a million pounds a year re-fitting lifts which didn't fit first time on site. More than that, they found five out of six lifts to have faults when assembled in the factory prior to shipping (a wasteful activity in itself). Everything worked to procedures but no one was learning; the means were obscured by the value placed on ISO 9000. There were plenty of procedures for dealing with non-conformance, none for how to learn.

The lift factory consumed more than 40 per cent of its revenue in waste — profits were poured down the drain. Emphasis on procedures was the wrong focus — it was a system which predictably produced waste and reported the same between functions, allocating blame.

While the managers at Laser Co. fought the excessive dogmatism of their ISO 9000 consultant, they nevertheless subscribed to the same traditional (functional) view. It is a view that results in documentation of how things "should" be done, when perhaps we first should be questioning why and how well things are done. It is true that in their case improvements were made through clarifying procedures. As we have said clarity is important — people need to know what their job is and why they are doing it — but clarity doesn't have to come with the encumbrances of bureaucracy and inspection.

Laser Co. will not improve from their current position without establishing operational measures derived from what matters to their customers; their focus should be value and flow. This is more than flow charting (a useful step beyond writing procedures); it is determining the "value stream" — the specific actions required to travel from an order through to finished product in the hands of a customer — and cutting out all waste (for example, time, materials and errors).

All traditionally managed manufacturing operations show large quantities of waste when viewed as a flow. The same problems are apparent in most of our service organisations: work is typically designed and managed as functional specialisms in the mistaken belief that optimising the parts — which usually means controlling costs — will optimise the whole. An example:

> Customers experiencing a fault on their computer equipment contact a call centre. The call centre's job is to log the call. The call is passed (as an electronic record) to the diagnostics function, whose job it is to call the customer back and determine the nature of the fault (is it hardware, software, application, network, etc.). Having made a decision the diagnostics group passes the call to the specified "expert" group who, effectively, cover the diagnostic work again and take remedial action. When one looks at the "value work" — the work required to be done to solve a problem — and compares it with what happened to each call, there is abundant waste and duplication. What's more, the whole system only gets it "right first time" for 30 per cent of the calls.

By understanding more about the nature of incoming calls (what types and how predictable?), they were able to move the decision-making — the value work — to the front end of this system, where customers called in. It improved service and reduced costs immediately because this cleaned the flow.[1]

A systems view of organisations leads to a different collection of problems to address. Managers who learn to take a systems view give up their preoccupation with budgetary or output data, management of activity and procedures and, most of all, they give up the idea of the division of "decision-making" (management's job) from "doing" (the worker's job). Instead, they work on the "causes of costs" — the way their system works to deliver what matters to their customers — and the means required to control and improve performance. It is an outside-in and "flow" view of the organisation instead of a top-down and "functional" view. From this point of view, the many conditions which have inhibited performance improvement (ISO 9000 registration being just one) become evident. Managers are faced with the task of removing the old ways of managing at the same time as introducing the new. This is not as daunting as it first appears, but it does require a different set of behaviours from managers. Remote, "by the numbers" management is replaced by hands-on, "value-flow" management. Leadership is, after all, the engine of change.

A better attitude to customers

Historically, one of ISO 9000's most damaging clauses has been the clause labelled "Contract Review". While the year 2000 revision has dropped this specific phrase, much of the same thinking remains.

Managers need to question whether a "contract" should be the focus for their relationship with customers. Perhaps it had some relevance for the provision of bombs in World War 2, perhaps it was appealing as a way to establish basic contractual controls over the performance of companies building or supplying to power stations and the like. But a contractual relation-

---

[1]   In this case the average time to solve customers' problems fell from six days to nine hours.

ship differs from a service, partnering or co-operative relationship. As we saw with Metal Co., the opportunities for partnering with customers (and suppliers) were lost through an obsession with contractual thinking. ISO 9000 is part of the current business-to-business relationship, contributing to a way of working which hinders mutual performance improvement. The work to be done to improve "joint processes" starts from a different attitude, but co-operation is less likely to occur in a contractual atmosphere.

In a similar way, ISO 9000 has caused organisations which supply directly to consumers to miss the point. How many of these customers require organisations to demonstrate anything other than *to be of service*? Customers want service to be "shaped" according to their demand, pure and simple. And if it is poor service, if it doesn't fit with or exceed their expectation, regardless of the reason, they will vote with their feet. There have been countless surveys which have shown that more than 70 per cent of customers who take their custom elsewhere do so because of a bad service experience.

In Lan Co. we saw how Contract Review increased the probability of a bad service experience. In Metal Co. we saw how the assessor explicitly advised action which would damage the relationship with the customer by unnecessary, over-bureaucratic emphasis on supplier control. In Tech Co. we saw how the Standard led to administrative attitudes which were defensive when dealing with customers — "we can prove what you ordered". Furthermore, it engendered greater conflict within their own company — "nothing moves without the right paperwork".

What was striking about the case studies — and in our experience is all too common in British organisations — is that with the exception of one department in one of the organisations, they had no idea what mattered to their customers, the starting point of a systems view. The exception was System Co.'s quotations department, which was delivering quotations at the time customers wanted them rather than to a standard. It is true that some of the cases (including Systems Co.) did customer surveys, but we have learned to treat customer surveys with extreme caution. Most often customer surveys focus on "how was it for you"; they do not tell us much about "what matters", and it is what matters which should drive the design of products and services. World class organisations are designed in such a way as to enable customers to "pull value" from them rather than "battle hard" to get what they want and then be expected to give a view on how it felt. The "how was it for you" type of customer survey hoodwinks managers into believing they are learning when they are not — learning starts by knowing what matters and how well an organisation responds to what matters. Systems Co. had been registered to ISO 9000 for a considerable time and had only just begun working on what mattered to their customers; it could have and should have been their first action. If understanding what mattered had been established for every point of transaction (not just quotations), and that had been followed by establishing internal, operational measures which illuminated how well they responded, they would have been able to improve performance.

The Standard had not encouraged these organisations to find out what mattered to their customers. Rather than facilitating improvement, Contract Review was a hindrance. It held up orders in Metal Co., it upset customers in Lan Co., it was translated into service standards — a major cause of waste — in Utility Co. Contract Review has been responsible for many of our service organisations becoming worse at providing service.

Metal Co. showed evidence of what appeared to matter to their customers — a plethora of surveys asking about their quality management system. Hence, like others, they were spurred into ISO 9000 registration by the fear of what might happen if they did not comply with the implicit or explicit requirement to register. There is little doubt that registration is not what actually mattered. These surveys were being generated by people who felt obliged to do as expected by their quality management system as defined and the definitive was governed by the Standard, consultants and assessors. The blind were coercing the dependent. Some refer to this phenomenon as the "ISO 9000 chain letter".

Just as ISO 9000 has coloured the business-to-business relationship, it has also affected the business-to-consumer relationship. We have seen many examples where bureaucracy has become a part of the service experience; consequently, the service experience has worsened. You find customers having to "work" the organisation to get what they want. Managers have decided what people "should do" in their various functions and, by implication, have decided what customers should expect when they transact with each function. It is the other side of "preventing non-conformity": decide what conformity is, what people should do. Many service organisations have been designed from this point of view. It is to worsen service and increase costs. An example from a correspondent will illustrate the problem:

> "I received an offer from a well-known credit card company. The essence of it was that, as a managing director of a company, they had chosen me as someone who should be a cardholder; they said they would not put me through hurdles as I was already "qualified"; and all I had to do was sign a form and they'd issue me with a company card. I thought 'great, I've heard so much about how good their service is and I'd like to try it for myself'. The card arrived. Then I realised that I had done something silly. I use another card for this business (the one they obviously got from a mailing list) and if I had thought about it, I should have asked for the new card to be put on my second business (a relatively new business, for which I needed a card). Being busy I just left it, not bothering to call (as asked) to 'activate' my card.
>
> Late one evening in the office, one of their people rang me. He was a personable young man. I was glad he called. I told him why I had not called to 'activate' and he said it would not be a problem, my card could be changed. Being very happy, I listened as he took me through what was obviously a script, the relevance of which I could not see (nothing they couldn't have told me before or later and had no bearing on the purpose of the call as I saw it). But I put up with the script because I was happy, I was going to get my problem solved. Then came my first shock. At the end of his script

the young man told me I should ring another number to solve my problem. I was not impressed and told him so. I told him what motivated me to become a customer in the first place. He assured me that I could expect better going forward. I rang the number and got my second shock — an IVR machine.[2] Of course I had to wait to the end to get the code for accessing a person and when I did so I got music. I waited for an interminable time, got through and was then told I had to fax this request to another number. My third shock. I gave up. Not happy. This should have been easy."

Reflect on this organisation. Was the young man being measured on the number of validations he did? He did not want the customer's need to get in his way; his managers were obviously not attuned to customer demands which went beyond what they had designed at this point of contact, other than perhaps issuing procedures instructing that these demands should be routed elsewhere (by the customer taking action). What did these managers know about the extent of calls which were outside of the intent they had designed, and did they consider the costs? What plans might they have had to redesign this service to make it better for the customer? Did they even think this way?

Had the managers responsible for the call centre justified the IVR machine on the basis of costs and productivity — passing the costs of call handling to the customer? Had they used anything more than traditional cost accounting to argue cost/benefit? What had been the impact of this innovation on the customer? How many customers dropped out of the IVR system? How many routed themselves to the "wrong" place? Were such data gathered? Were they usable for decision-making? This organisation exemplified traditional, "command and control" managerial precepts, their system will be bound to be sub-optimised. Is this why they are marketing to people like our correspondent? Are they losing customers? If they are, it is easy to see why.

When organisations are designed this way, customers are implicitly expected to be content being dealt with according to

---

[2] IVR = interactive voice response.

the activities prescribed (by managers). The "ISO 9000 view" is to assume that any non-conformance will be detected and "managed". However, a non-conformance in ISO 9000 terms is likely to be thought of as an operator doing something wrong — failing to follow a procedure. The more important "non-conformance" is the failure of the system to respond to a customer demand — these failures will only show up as complaints, yet most customers will not bother to complain, they'll just walk away.

The advocates of ISO 9000 argue that adherence to procedures assures control. This is to assume that control of procedures will ensure no variation in performance. However, there are always many sources of variation. When you look at an organisation from the customers' point of view (outside-in), it is easy to see how control of procedures will always increase variation (and thus worsen control). Why? Because customers' demands are customer-shaped, not necessarily procedures-shaped. And if an organisation is not customer-shaped it will inevitably take longer to deal with certain demands, deal with them less efficiently and get more complaints.

The language of the Standard encourages managers to think about complaints in terms of documentation and corrective action. So often, in our experience, the consequence is that all non-conformances are treated as though they are "common-cause", as if they are predictable and caused by the system. The result is, potentially, a proliferation of procedures that may have been unnecessary. If the event was, in fact, a "special cause", a "one-off", a new control would now delay the whole system. The failure to distinguish between "common-cause" and "special-cause" variation is usually manifest as "just in case" thinking. The returned goods example from Tech Co. is an extreme example of it and, as we saw, it is not a good idea to proceduralise something that is unpredictable. The same error has been institutionalised in some larger organisations through document control on their IT systems — the electronic complaint procedure obliges the worker to treat special causes as though they are common causes and thus establish new procedures (through *corrective actions*) which only worsen the situation.

The focus on complaints is the wrong focus. A better attitude to customers starts with knowing what matters to them and turning the same into operational measures. How else could one improve in the eyes of one's customers?

A better way of decision-making

What we saw in the case studies was that the "command and control" mentality of our current management mind-set was attracted to the idea that work should be controlled by creating, documenting and inspecting procedures. In Systems Co., this meant inspection of their procedures as defined (in functions). This is not the same as understanding how well they worked; improvement needed different thinking and different data. If they had worked on how well their processes delivered what mattered to customers and had employed capability data, showing how well they achieved it instead of relying on financial (cost) data, they would have had the means to learn how to improve — they could have made better decisions. As a corollary, if these better measures had been in the hands of people doing the work, their workforce could have been making decisions — learning and continuously improving service to their customers. Instead, the same headaches were experienced by the engineers, all problems of "design" not coinciding with "delivery". It is a perennial problem of traditional, functional, cost-based decision-making.

Decision-making in the thinking of the Standard centres around "do we do as we say we do?". In organisations which have been designed as functional hierarchies, registration to ISO 9000 "locks in" the waste by making it "invisible"; probably the most compelling reason to give up ISO 9000. What *is* visible becomes the focus of decision-making; it is defined by what is written about in manuals of procedures. It is the stuff of the inspector's work. The focus becomes meeting the requirements of inspection, not understanding and improving performance. As we saw in Metal Co., this results in unnecessary inspection and decisions about requirements for inspection being made by the assessor. It is no surprise that people object to their assessor's view of requirements; sometimes they just do not make good sense. In Lan Co. we saw how the assessor was argumentative, despite the fact that Lan Co.'s customers were suffering from the excesses of his strictures. He took an attitude of "catching them doing something wrong", which led in turn to the owner getting his people out of the way when the assessor was coming, something we have had reported to us by many correspondents. People can't be "found out" if they are not there.

Being "found out" is akin to being managed by "attention to output", the primary means of decision-making in "command and control" organisations. In all of the case studies and in most organisations we work with, management by "output data" is the norm, the order of the day. The problem is that attention to output inhibits learning. It only encourages people to do what they have to do to "meet the number" or "pass the assessment". We also observed how this phenomenon distorted the measurement and reporting of service standards in Utility Co. People had to do whatever they could to avoid getting grief from management and management sought to avoid grief from the regulator. If, for each of the customer transactions defined as service "guarantees", they had known their capability — what they currently predictably achieve — and had set to work on the causes of variation, people might have been motivated, contributing and learning. As it was, people were demoralised and the system was not improving. It could not improve; the means for improvement were out of the hands of management. If the utility companies are to be obliged to report to regulators, they would be far better off reporting their capability and investing their efforts and resources on improving it. Their current system (guarantees, refunds and associated reporting bureaucracy) is all additional cost and cannot be considered a foundation for improvement. To know how to improve would require measures of capability and work on the causes of waste and variation. The choice of measures should be driven by what matters to customers, and that is unlikely to be "having to fill in forms and receive financial compensation" when things go wrong.

In the language of the Standard, process management is not about establishing capability and learning from variation. The ISO 9000 philosophy is that work should be planned and then controlled according to the plan. It appears plausible, but it is at the root of the problem. Organisations and managers assume, *a priori*, that the right way (of working) can be decided, *a priori*, whether by managers or the people doing the work. It is a far more effective strategy to assume that the first step in quality improvement is to understand how well the system or process works currently, before documenting or controlling anything. This is to start at "check" or "study" rather than "plan". Reflecting its antecedents, ISO 9000 values control over learning.

The Standard places great emphasis on inspection and testing throughout the production process. Many studies have shown that inspection only increases errors. The whole philosophy of quality by inspection is based on the assumption that decision-making should be separated from work. It is diametrically opposed to quality by making improvement through giving control to operators and learning how to reduce variation — the latter philosophy of quality empowers the individual, the former does not.

Probably the single biggest influence on the bureaucratisation associated with ISO 9000 is the clause on document control. The Standard requires documents to be controlled and procedures to be established for making changes to documents. No wonder, when confronted with the consequences of these obligations, people question whether these requirements are doing anything to improve performance in the organisation or simply enabling the inspectors to do their job.

ISO 9000 is an artefact of "command and control" thinking. It ensures that what is written into the quality system is a philosophy of control and inspection; decision-making is separated from work. It is an approach which leads to decisions focused on whether people work as planned — not whether the system is being managed for improvement.

One correspondent put it this way:

"After five years of ISO 9000 I have come to the view that it is about compliance, not quality. It doesn't really drive improvement. We thought we needed consistency to get improvement started and maybe we did but ISO 9000 made us look at consistency and conformity, variance from what should have happened was treated as important. We now know it would have been more useful to learn from variation, something we discovered only recently. ISO 9000 has been de-motivational. It is not about 'faster, more efficiency, trying things' and so on, it is about 'do it this way and record failure'. It's like getting a bad report at school."

This is the entry point — its the first thing managers focus on — what do we have to write down to satisfy the assessor? Managers would be far better off addressing a different question: how well does it work at the moment? If these organisations had understood what mattered to their customers and turned the same into operational measures, they could have established methods of working which would have resulted in understanding, and hence improvement.

A better way of measurement

Measures should be derived from purpose. In Tech Co. the purpose of the organisation was to sell and deliver products to customers. Knowing how well they did this (capability) and how predictably they worked (variation) would have been a better starting place for improvement than controlling people's behaviour through procedures. Similarly, Systems Co. should have been concerned with measures of their ability to ship and fit what the customers wanted without experiencing failures. Measures derived from purpose help managers to focus their action on the system.

Improvement is achieved through redesigning the way the process works or reducing variation. Managers who have no idea of the theory of variation should take a set of numbers they often use for decision-making and put them into a control chart.[3] If managers accept the theory of variation — that a system or

---

[3] Resources for calculating control charts are available from www.lean-service.com.

process can be expected to produce values between the upper and lower limits unless something extraordinary happens — the first thing they usually learn (in our experience of "command and control" organisations) is that the process is stable but it shows wide variation. When you know that you can expect to get values at any point between the upper and lower control limits, and too many values at the lower end would put you way under budget, it makes you stop and think. The variation in values is caused by the system, not the people. Clearly there is no point in paying attention to people. It is a compelling argument for finding out more about the system.

Sometimes wide variation in measures of a system is caused by the measure being representative of a number of processes. For example, sales data might relate to a number of sales processes. So it is helpful to obtain data for each of the processes, which should be considered separately. In many organisations obtaining data of this sort takes a little time, demonstrating how removed they are from sources of data for improvement. It is also frequently the case that management actions ("paying attention to output") cause widening variation — people pull data forwards or backwards to be seen to "meet their numbers". They comply with work standards or targets regardless of the impact on service, efficiency or revenue. When managers see the consequences of their decisions through seeing data over time it can have a profound effect on the way they subsequently think and manage. Measures of variation help managers decide whether a process should be redesigned or continually improved (they often need both, a number of times).

Utility Co. showed just how damaging the whole idea of work standards can be when they are translated into customer service guarantees. The "Contract Review" mentality was evident — "we tell you what we will do and you have means of redress if we don't do it" — and the consequences for the organisation and customers were devastating. It is an object lesson to all who believe that service standards are a good thing. Standards are anathema to quality — they always cause suboptimisation. Guarantees and other forms of work standards appear attractive because they give managers something to "manage". They are similar numbers to the usual functional budget numbers and are reported in similar ways (this week versus last week). In each of the case studies we saw how managers were used to managing with output data (activity and budgets) and setting standards or targets. Few realise how managing this way causes sub-optimisation.

Better measures start with a different view. Take, for example, Laser Co. Using measures of time — a process measure — might have had a profound impact on quality and service. At the very least, this would have alerted management to the difference between "value time" (the time taken to make a product) and the total time products spent in the organisation. But managers don't usually look for these things. Instead they are generally preoccupied with functional measures such as measures of activity; they assume that more activity must result in more productivity. This is not true. We work to the general principle that when we find managers managing activity we will always find sub-optimisation as a consequence; never have we found evidence to the contrary. ISO 9000 reinforces this thinking; things that can be measured (activity) can be managed. It is not the way to improve performance. To improve performance you need measures of capability and variation in relation to what matters to customers. They lead to better decisions. It is the same thinking that informs how best to work with suppliers.

A better attitude to suppliers

For the first 15 years the purchasing clause in ISO 9000 required organisations to select sub-contractors on the basis of their *ability to meet sub-contract requirements, including quality requirements* — it reminds us of the plumber, reported in a national newspaper, who was reported as using his friend as a sub-contractor "because he's good" but who was found to be non-conformant by his assessor because the assessor wanted documentary proof. The plumber could not get over the idea that he had to write down that "Joe" would be used as a sub-contractor "because he was good". In the 1994 review, the purchasing clause was extended to emphasise the evaluation of suppliers in respect of their *quality system and any specific quality assurance requirements;* increasing the probability that organisations will do the easy thing and insist all suppliers are registered to ISO 9000, regardless of the impact on performance.

The proliferation of supplier assessment questionnaires has continued. Another crazy example:

> In 1992 we published a book called *I Want You to Cheat.* People in organisations bought the book and thus we appeared on "supplier lists". Once our company name became visible to someone responsible for exercising the purchasing clause of ISO 9000, we would be sent a supplier questionnaire asking us about our quality system. All for having sold a book to someone in the organisation for £11.00.

Suppliers usually regard such questionnaires as a threat — in our case it was just daft — and the most common consequence is that people feel they ought to do whatever it takes to get registered. As we have shown, coercion is unlikely to establish learning and improvement. Instead it fosters "cheating", people doing anything to avoid being found out and — fear of fears — risk losing registration, despite the fact that there is no evidence to suggest that organisations lose out if they de-register.

Metal Co. showed how they "cheated" to prevent the assessor "catching them out" using a "non-authorised" supplier. Where they thought the evaluation of suppliers to be important they acted, but in practice, as we saw, they were actually having to control supplier product because suppliers were nervous about publishing their quality data. A competitive rather than co-operative attitude.

It was interesting to note the different attitudes to quality between Metal Co.'s customers. The British saw ISO 9000 as an entry point, whereas the Japanese began the relationship by working on common processes and were indifferent to ISO 9000. Which behaviour reflected a better understanding of and approach to quality? Metal Co. could have made great strides for improvement if they had been working co-operatively with their suppliers and customers. ISO 9000 reinforced an alternative, "contractual" regime. In their case, increased inventory was an obvious symptom, adding costs throughout the value chain and hampering flow.

One might argue that sectors such as civil engineering and munitions supply need contracts between supplier and customer. The construction sector has trumpeted the need for change from its contractual, adversarial relations for the last ten years. But it is a sector whose system is designed to maintain adversarial behaviour between contracting parties: there are armies of independent professionals who earn money from squeezing suppliers against the terms of their contracts. The gains made by the independent professionals and the extra costs borne by both parties are all costs to the system. A quality approach would be to work together for mutual benefit. Contractual thinking begets adversarial relations; in turn, this prevents learning. ISO 9000 has the wrong ethos.

The resultant ethos

The Standard's ethos is to assume, *a priori*, that documentation and control of people's behaviour in procedures will prevent problems. Yet there is no evidence to support this view. It is a control ethos, not an improvement ethos. It further assumes that you can't trust people — staff or customers. A focus on procedures leads to people behaving in ways which value procedures over purpose (whether they like it or not). It is easy to see how ISO 9000 registration can lead to demoralisation and a deficit in learning.

The ethos we need is not what should we do, but how can we learn? Improvement starts with being prepared to change thinking. When organisations are run on command and control principles, the numbers in use do not easily facilitate learning; they tell you more about what has happened than what is happening and why. Worse, the data in use usually cause suboptimisation: people work to make their numbers or standards at the expense of the system. Taking a systems view shows the extent to which command and control management causes suboptimisation. It is a powerful source of motivation for change.

An improvement ethos starts with "what matters to customers?" From there we would need to learn about how well the current system responds to "what matters" — and to what extent the current response is predictable. It is to look outside-in, and from that perspective seek to understand what is happening predictably with respect to "demand" and "response". How well do we deliver product or service according to what matters to the customers, how well do we respond to the various demands they make on our system? How predictable are the demands customers make and what causes them? What are the things that we currently do that help or hinder our performance? Taking a systems view leads to improvement.

Taking a systems view is the first step in understanding — it teaches managers about the "what and why" of performance. It is of more value then using output data ("driving by looking through the rear-view mirror").

A professional services organisation with 55 branches was being assailed with complaints by a major customer for the inaccuracy of their work. In desperation they decided to set up a central team to check all the work, which meant all branches submitting their work to Head Office rather than directly to the customer. Quality improved only slightly; more than 50 per cent of the work showed errors and many errors still 'got through' the Head Office net. Top management had been attracted by the notion of ISO 9000, believing that consistency was their problem ("it would work fine if everybody did as they should") and that was what the Standard was aimed at. It was also considered advantageous from a marketing point of view to be registered to ISO 9000.

An ISO 9000 consultant was shown their problem and he agreed that it was grist to the ISO 9000 mill. His recommendation was to review the procedural material and establish clear responsibilities for what was to be done at each step in the procedures and how the work should be checked. Quite sensibly, the consultant advised an analysis of errors to identify the most common and to ensure that the new procedures were written to be as "idiot-proof" as possible with these errors in mind. A central team was established to write procedures based on the customer requirements. They started work by tracking a series of cases through the system from and back to the customer. It was clear that the quality of the instructions from the Head Office were one cause of errors — they were ambiguous, in different formats and amended by badly worded (not easy to assimilate) updates. It would have been plausible at that stage to believe that the problem had been identified and without doubt a "control of procedures" approach might have achieved some improvement with better instructions and better controlled documentation. However, as the intrepid investigators proceeded, someone had a different thought. There were, she observed, more fundamental problems.

The work procedures were split into technical and support work — the technical work was performed by the professionals and the administrative work, for example, typing, was performed by office-based staff. Whilst observing work going through branches she noted that the people who did the technical work were handling cases entirely unaided; they had their own personal case load. (And, as it happens, they were measured on the number of cases completed and ones outstanding.) Their work entailed being out on the road, remembering all the detailed requirements for many different customers and coping with a large amount of "work in progress". This was, she observed, due to the historical structure of the organisation; something which perhaps needed to be re-considered from a "demand" or "flow" point of view. The way work was currently being done had never been adjusted while new and more complex demands were made on the system. She came to the view that the fundamental structure was the problem; no matter how good the instructions were, the complexity being handled by the technical experts would mean they were never going to produce accurate work. In simple terms, it is very difficult to get hundreds of people, spread all over the country, to handle a variety of tools in the same way — especially when the requirements keep changing. The current system included third-party inspection and double-checking, so the "procedures" route would only be likely to augment what was already a poor work system. It needed a radical rethink.

The team realised that their best strategy was to find a way to control all of the work as it came in from customers. They realised that they needed to put their very best resource on the front end to "clean up" and organise the customers' cases as they hit the organisation. The technical and administrative staff needed to be integrated and control of the work flow given to administrators. This would leave the technical people free to apply the skills that they were paid for. The measurement system had to change to measure flow rather than volume and revenue (they knew that if flow improved, service would improve and thus improvements in revenue and volume would follow).

It didn't stop there. They got engaged with one of their customers in looking at the whole process — beginning to end — from the customer's point of view and made changes to the way they worked together which improved the efficiency of both operations and improved service to the customer.

The question is: what is there in ISO 9000 that would have encouraged this organisation to think the way they needed to? Working to procedures would have been to treat the symptoms with no guarantee of not making the patient worse; the solution lay in understanding the organisation as a system, something not common amongst ISO 9000 assessors and consultants.

A systems philosophy is at the heart of the Vanguard Standards (published at www.lean-systems.com). Some people claim that a systems philosophy is embedded in the revised Standard (ISO 9000: 2000). We disagree. The revision does represent a move in that direction, but much traditional thinking remains. In Chapter 9 we discuss the new Standard, but first we take a look at the process used to review and improve the Standard and question whether it was likely to result in an improvement.

Chapter 8

THE ISO 9000 REVIEW:
A PROCESS OF IMPROVEMENT?

The year 2000 revision of ISO 9000 is expected, at the time of writing, to be published in November 2000. This version of the Standard has become widely known as ISO 9000: 2000. The process of the revision has been described as "continuous improvement". We will discuss the extent to which this new Standard represents an improvement in Chapter 9, but first we need to inspect the improvement process and ask how well it was likely to achieve its purpose.

The body responsible for revisions is ISO Technical Committee 176. In 1997, TC 176 declared itself to be listening to the "voice of the customer". In *Quality Online*[1] TC 176 was reported as having learned from its customers that ISO 9000 registration needs to "improve confidence in outcomes and value relative to the implementation effort". In plain language this can only mean customers were worried about whether it works — improves performance — and whether it is worth the effort. The customers were also reported as saying that the review needs to "improve applicability to a broad range of organisational sizes and range of products" and needs to "improve flexibility of use and user-friendliness". These needs indicate customers were having problems. It is no more or less than a declaration that ISO 9000 suffers problems of interpretation and value-in-use.

TC 176 published its vision and mission statements:

---

[1] January 1997, http://www.qualitymag.com.

"Our vision is that, through its worldwide acceptance and use, the ISO 9000 family of standards will provide an effective means for improving the performance of individual organisations and providing confidence to people and organisations that products (goods and services) will meet their expectations thereby enhancing trade, global prosperity, and individual well-being."

The mission is to:

"Identify and understand user needs in the field of quality management, develop standards that respond effectively to the expectations of users, support implementation of these standards, and facilitate meaningful evaluation of the resulting implementations."

There is an explicit assumption that ISO 9000 is here to stay. If TC 176 were really listening to their customers, would there not be a stronger emphasis on *meaningful evaluation of implementation*? If there were, perhaps they would come to the conclusion that their vision is inappropriate, for standards do not provide the most *effective means* for improving the performance of organisations.

Just suppose for a moment that ISO 9000 was a product. Would it be reflective of a quality attitude to keep obliging people to buy a product when the users complain of cost-effectiveness and usability? If the marketplace obligation were ceased, we are confident that this "product" would die a natural death for there is little intrinsic value to the customer. Each time the Standard has been revised, the critics have maintained that it continues to show the same weaknesses — that it is too unfriendly to use, leads to too much bureaucracy and is too strongly influenced by assessors who show poor understanding of how to run a business. You would have thought these criticisms alone would be enough to call a halt to the promulgation of the Standard as a necessary condition for doing business.

Shouldn't TC 176 be working on why there are problems of these kinds? Isn't this where *meaningful evaluation of implementation* would be of value? When TC 176 met for a week in

Tel Aviv[2] in November 1996, the same period in which they published their vision and mission, they did not spend their time discussing the value of implementation, they spent their time discussing how to converge the various standards. Convergence of ISO 9002 and ISO 9003 with ISO 9001; convergence of QS 9000 with ISO 9000; convergence of ISO 9000 with ISO 14000 (the environmental standard). TC 176 claims to be listening to its customers but spends its time on other issues — convergence will not solve the problems of cost-effectiveness and usability, and may even compound them.

TC 176 spends time on convergence because it is the stuff of the standards movement; it is what they exist to do. As new standards are being developed for health and safety and environmental issues, the revisionists want to incorporate them all into general standards for doing business. Where is the evidence that shows us this is a sensible thing to do? We fear that convergence will result in building a larger army of more broadly based and thus even less competent assessors. Inspection will take over as a way of doing business. The likely impact of this on the performance of organisations is catastrophic.

A lesson in poor change management?

TC 176 managed to ignore the impact of its decisions because it began its work from the assumption that standards are here to stay. It began at "plan" — decide what to do — rather than "check" — learn how well it currently works. Their purpose was how to manage the revision of ISO 9000, not question its value. To achieve their purpose, TC 176 created a project management structure. This is illustrative of a "command and control" approach to change management — decide what you want to achieve, break it into parts, manage the deliverables and inter-dependencies. Project managers responsible for the whole and the parts created plans, then executed the plans. The systems thinker would have started at "check", understanding

---

[2] The players involved in the various review committees have travelled the world in their endeavours. This year they have met in San Francisco and Kyoto.

the what and why of current performance. It would, no doubt, have led to entirely different conclusions and actions.

This was the structure used for the change process:

Figure 8.1 The Change Management Structure

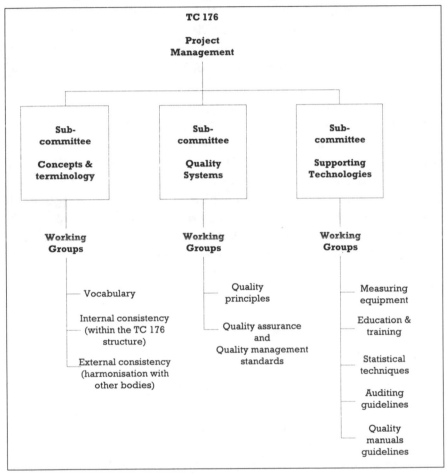

Imagine the problems faced by such a structure. The working group responsible for the new standards would have been dependent on those responsible for definitions, the working group responsible for guidance for auditors would be dependent on everybody, the group responsible for internal liaison would be trying to ensure people talk to each other with a consistent language. And of course disputes would be bound to occur. For example, our informants told us that the group responsible for terminology chose to use the term "products" to mean products and services. However, the group responsible for writing the standards insisted on differentiating products and services. The horse-trading that subsequently occurred represented internally focused energy, it is a natural consequence of the organisation design.

When we first saw this structure it reminded us of a similar structure being used by an IT organisation to change its service operation. In just the same way the project mentality and strucure led to an abundance of waste (internally) and, moreover, resulted in a plan and actions that did not improve the operations. When we took them through a better methodology — based on "check" — they improved performance in weeks. The project management structure had been in place for a year.[3]

Similarly, the TC 176 project management structure has been in place for years. We shall focus in particular on the working group responsible for rewriting the Standard.

A lesson in how not to run a survey?

The working group responsible for rewriting the Standard decided to conduct a survey of users' requirements.[4] The first thing that has to be said about the survey is that the recipients were the wrong people! They were not senior line managers of organisations registered to ISO 9000. They were not customers of organisations registered to ISO 9000. The survey was distributed to national standards bodies, national accreditation bodies and accredited certification and registration bodies. In other words, it was distributed amongst those who have an interest in maintaining the ISO 9000 infrastructure. From these institutions, the survey was passed on to people in organisations. The majority of these respondents were quality managers, auditors and quality consultants — people who have a vested interest in maintaining ISO 9000. Despite this bias in the data, the survey results were illuminating.

The main findings of this survey were:

---

[3] This was the case reported in Chapter 7, where time to fix fell from an average of six days to nine hours.

[4] The report of this survey is published at www.iso.ch/presse/user.htm.

Harmonisation: People wanted harmonisation of ISO 9000 with ISO 14000 (the environmental standard).

Tailoring: People wanted to be able to omit some requirements of the Standard if they thought it inappropriate for their organisation, but the respondents also wanted guidance on this.

Continuous improvement: People wanted a demonstration of continuous improvement to be a requirement of the Standard.

User friendliness: People wanted the Standard to be simpler to use, clearer in language and more easily understood.

Process orientation: People wanted the quality management system to be described as a process rather than being solely a set of (20) requirements.

This is the voice of the partisan user saying there is room for improvement. The process of the survey ensured that the ISO 9000 institution fed its own "de-facto" purpose — maintaining the ISO 9000 institutions. The working group responsible for the survey did what was expected of them — they conducted a survey asking for views about how the Standard could be improved. They did not ask whether ISO 9000 was a valuable contribution to economic performance; this was assumed. The discontent in their respondents, people who have a vested interest, continued. At the time of writing we were told that more than 200 "negative" comments from UK users are with the UK sub-committee responsible for feeding views through to the review committee. This committee had to "accept" or "reject" them, and pass their findings up the reviewing hierarchy. Insiders told us that while this put a break on the process leading up to the publication of the new Standard, it could never have stopped it. Too many vested interests would not have been served if the UK committee had refused to endorse the revision.

Not only did the survey address a partisan audience, it did so with leading questions, for example:

Should the quality management system described in the QA and QM standards be based on a process model of an organisation (rather than being based solely on a set of requirements like the 20 ISO 9001 paragraphs of today)?

Should the QA and QM standards be suitable for an easy integration of quality management with other management aspects of a company's business (e.g. environment, finance, health and safety)?

Should the ISO 9000 and ISO 14000 series standards be more compatible?

Should users be able to exclude requirements of the QA standards that do not apply to them?

Should it be a requirement of the QA standard to demonstrate continuous improvement?

Is it important for you that the pair of QA and QM standards should be clear in language?

Is it important for you that the pair of QA and QM standards should be simple to use?

. . . and so on.

We find it difficult to understand how a minority (for it was only that) of respondents actually said no to any of the above. All would serve their interests. This community followed its interest while criticising its past. Harmonisation would lead to more work for inspectors. More scope in interpretation would create the need for more advice. The requirements for continuous improvement and a process orientation create the need for more training. But how does this community think about continuous improvement and will the training to be provided help or hinder?

The survey should have been focused on the question, "Does ISO 9000 work?" But such a survey would have fallen foul of the phenomenon we found in our 1993 survey of opinion. People cannot be relied upon to present reliable data. Beside the prejudice to maintain the ISO 9000 infrastructure, and their role in it, they are more likely to rationalise the benefits of standards — it is hard to accept that years of effort are worth little, so people make claims for benefits without any data to support the claims. A better method of research might have been to follow the route we took with case studies. We are confident that the same results would have been found — that ISO 9000 predictably causes sub-optimisation. Its implicit theory, advice regarding, and interpretation of the clauses being at the centre of the problems.

Such an analysis would certainly call for a more significant rewrite of the Standard.

A lesson in how not to rewrite a standard?

TC 176 sought views on how to rewrite the Standard. They followed the procedures laid down by the International Standards Organisation for the rewriting of any standard. While successive drafts were described as drafts for public comment, the process was unlikely to be receptive to or accommodate public comment. The committee responsible for the redrafting of ISO 9000 would only accept comments submitted by member bodies and recognised liaison organisations. Should any individual have wished to submit comments, these had to be directed to a Member Body or recognised Liaison Organisation. Member Bodies are, effectively, each nation's "Standards Institution" and Liaison Organisations are, typically, assessing organisations and associations of assessors and the like. Once again, the organisations involved are populated with people who have a vested and often pecuniary interest in maintaining ISO 9000 as a requirement for doing business. The only provision for outsiders to influence this community was for them to represent views to a sub-level of the decision-making process in the hope that the views would be passed on and subsequently listened to by the committee. (As a matter of record, we submitted our views on the first re-drafting of ISO 9000 to a British Liaison Organisation. We could find no evidence they had been listened to or understood in the subsequent drafts. That might not surprise you.)

The review process has caused confusion (by design)

In its notes accompanying the second draft, the committee noted that "a number of member bodies had submitted a series of contradictory comments against specific clauses". This should be no surprise. If we take a step back from the exercise, what do we see? A large number of people who are involved in the standards movement, with differing life experiences, expressing their views of how the Standard should be interpreted in practice. It is hardly likely that this process would produce a consensus. So what did those responsible for the review do to resolve the confusion? They established a procedure. This has to be the best quality joke of the millennium.[5] Any submission had to be on a template — a form — where the reviewer had to identify the clause, suggest some other words and then justify that suggestion.

This appears rational. However, its rationality is its Achilles heal, for implicit is the assumption that the players share a common view of the world. Furthermore, without any objective evidence about what works, the exercise descended into what can be agreed through this process amongst interested but disparate parties. The consequence is confusion. ISO 9000: 2000 is both confused and confusing. This is the fault of the review process — it is designed in. On the one hand the new Standard talks about systems thinking and on the other it specifically encourages practices that are anything but. Perhaps it reflects the state of learning amongst the ISO 9000 community, but surely this should not be allowed to dictate the design and management of our organisations?

Lack of any criterion or objectivity about what works

The review process assumes, *a priori*, that ISO 9000 "works". But where is the evidence? In our own research we found that ISO 9000 registration predictably had two effects: Firstly, it caused organisations to do things that were bad for business,

---

[5] To establish a procedure in such circumstances will only ensure greater variation in the output, as has been the case.

and secondly, it stopped organisations seeing and acting on things that would make them better.

If we were asked to address the question, "What do we know about what works?", we would think of three sources: Warwick Business School research into small and medium-sized businesses (SMEs), the success of many Japanese manufacturers and our own clients who have made use of systems thinking in the design and management of their operations. Leaving aside our clients, what objective evidence do we have about what works?

What works in SMEs?

The research published by Warwick Business School uses an analogy to summarise its findings: There are two ways of getting a boat swiftly down river. You can work on getting the crew to work better together, or you can get the boat into a faster current and let the current do the work. The latter strategy, the research shows, is the secret of business success.

The Warwick research shows that successful companies didn't have concern for tidy procedures, they were not following any of the government-promulgated initiatives (ISO 9000, Investors in people, Business Excellence — equivalent to the Baldrige Award in the US — benchmarking and so on). But what they did instead was simple: They identified a market niche that was growing rapidly and jumped in to exploit it. Such niche opportunities are thrown up by change — technological, social or legislative. Pre-cooked and pre-packaged food, customised holidays, newly privatised services, and specialised services, for example, spectacles in an hour, are just some examples where companies have established fast growth where nothing much existed before.

The second major finding was that these companies listened very hard to their customers, especially in terms of what they were doing and what they would like to do with the service or product. From the customers' point of view, the service or product solves a problem, fills a need; it does something of value. Knowing what that is, is critical to staying ahead; ensuring that future product development puts the customers problems at the forefront.

And these, according to the research, are the two secrets of success — exploit a growing niche and listen to and learn from customers. Could any kind of standard help? A standard could say nothing about the existence of a market niche, but it might provide method for the latter — how one uses customer data to drive operations and product/service design. But ISO 9000 is not regarded as the "hot ticket" for the design of service operations. Why? Because, despite the claims for the revision, it remains an internally focused instrument. A systems view would have started with customer demand, it would have sought to understand the value work — what mattered to customers — and it would have sought to understand and manage flow. Things the new standard does not talk about.

What worked in Japanese manufacturers?

Since 1950 some manufacturers in Japan have been outstripping the industrial performance of their Western counterparts by significant amounts. Of particular note is the Toyota Production System. Research shows the Toyota Production System to be vastly superior to other manufacturing systems in terms of cost and quality. The Toyota Production System takes a wholly different view of the design and management of work, being based on systems principles. Similarly, we might look to the production methods of Mitsubishi where documentary evidence points to superiority of method. Again, the principles and practices are based on systems thinking and the management of flow rather than function.

In our most recent round of case studies, conducted with Takaji Nishizawa, we found that the few who were using methods originally developed by Toyota were doing so in spite of ISO 9000 registration. Furthermore, they were keeping these methods out of their quality management system so as not to cause issues with their assessors. It is ironic that the means for improvement are kept separate from registration to the Standard. However, it is understandable when one appreciates that the ISO 9000 assessor does not start from the question "what works?".

How well did the process achieve its purpose?

The purpose of the review was to improve ISO 9000, to make ISO 9000 better with respect to its purpose — to improve the economic performance of organisations. However, the review included no criterion reference — no work was done on what "good" looks like, on what works. There was no research on the value of the Standard in use. The process limited the collection of views to those who had an interest in the Standard. The review was conducted through a project management structure, it was change by "plan", it was to assume that the parties would collectively get to the right answer.

Inevitably the process led to confusion and the confusion was "managed" by a mixture of bureaucracy and procedures. It should be no surprise that the resultant Standards have shortcomings. There is no evidence to suggest that these Standards will be an improvement and plenty of evidence to suggest that ISO 9000 may have dug its own grave. While the espoused purpose of the review has been to improve the Standard, the de facto purpose has been to maintain its institutions.

Marketplace coercion will, no doubt, continue to be the major influence on the continued use of ISO 9000. The revision, if it has resulted in a better Standard, may be considered by some to have made the Standard more useful. To assess its value we now turn to our critique of the new Standard.

Chapter 9

ISO 9000: 2000 — A CRITIQUE

It must be said at the outset that this has been a major and fundamental review of ISO 9000. The title has changed, it is now "Quality Management Systems — Requirements", and no longer includes the term "Quality Assurance", marking a final move away from its "control" antecedents and making a clear assertion that this is now to be regarded as an "improvement" tool. There are no longer 20 clauses. Instead, the new Standard has eight clauses: Scope, Normative Reference, Terms and Definitions, Quality Management System Requirements, Management Responsibility, Resource Management, Product and/or Service Realisation and Measurement, Analysis and Improvement.

The new Standard is no longer treated as "one size fits all". Reflecting, no doubt, the historic criticisms, ISO 9001: 2000 clearly states that, "It is not the purpose . . . to imply uniformity in the structure of quality management systems or uniformity of documents".[1] Thus the user has some degree of freedom to choose what to do and how to do it. Furthermore, the new Standard includes a sub-clause permitting exclusions. The historic criticisms were, no doubt, caused by the original Standard's application — the principles and practices for managing munitions manufacturing and power generation, for example, are unlikely to be universally applicable to a wide variety of organisations. It is disturbing that it has taken us 20 years or more to learn that.

---

[1] In this chapter we quote from the last Draft International Standard, as the final version of ISO 9000: 2000 was not available at the time of writing. However, we are confident that the final version will be much the same — the review process itself precludes any major changes. The quotations from the draft are reproduced with permission.

ISO 9000: 2000 is described as a "consistent pair" of Standards. ISO 9001: 2000 is the Standard against which an organisation will be assessed — it states quality management system "requirements". ISO 9004: 2000 gives "guidance on the application of quality management". However, ISO 9004: 2000 is not intended as guidance for compliance with ISO 9001: 2000. To put this another way, you can follow the guidance in 9004 but you will be assessed against 9001.

In our view, these are not a "consistent pair"; the content, if you read it as a systems thinker, is confused and confusing. We have argued (Chapter 8) that this is a fault of the process. Our critique of ISO 9000: 2000 is based on the question, "How well does this revision represent and encourage systems thinking in organisations?" Our answer is not sufficiently well. ISO 9000: 2000 does use the word "system" and does talk about the need for the organisation to be managed as a system. However, the principles and practices as represented by the eight clauses fit more comfortably with what might be called the traditional "command and control" perspective on the design and management of work. While a lot has changed in terms of content, not enough has changed in terms of substance.

Having said that, the year 2000 review looks likely to provide for greater scope in interpretation and use. For the first time the user could interpret and apply the Standard from a systems perspective. If the user were to do so, this would need to be argued with the assessor.

The detail of the new Standard has yet to be finalised. We understand from those who are close to the revision committees that the debate, at this late stage, continues between the traditionalists and the modernisers. The traditionalists favour documentation as the principle means of inspection while the modernisers argue, as we do, that organisations should choose where documentation is vital in their specific circumstances and where it is better to control work by other means, latitude for interpretation should be provided. The implication is that inspection may require assessors to understand more about the work, rather than rely on the evidence provided by documents and records.

At the time of writing it is not certain what the final version of ISO 9000: 2000 will say, so in this chapter we will discuss the theory and practice advocated by ISO 9000: 2000 by reference to the Standard's eight quality management principles:[2]

- Customer focus

- Leadership

- Involvement of people

- Process approach

- System approach to management

- Continual improvement

- Factual approach to decision-making, and

- Mutually beneficial supplier relationships.

These, at first reading, appear to be a positive step forward in as much as one could take a systems perspective to interpreting each and all. However, a systems interpretation of these principles is not what informs the Standard's documents. In many respects, the Standard is either insufficient or misleading in the way it treats performance improvement, perhaps an inevitable consequence of having its parts written by disparate parties.

In our critique of the revision, we are asking, "How well does this revision represent and encourage systems thinking in organisations?" When we review the Standard we are looking for encouragement of specific things; to help the reader here is a re-cap of the fundamentals of systems thinking.

Fundamentals of systems thinking

Outside-in. Rather than treating the organisation as a top-down hierarchy, it is better to understand it from the customers' point

---

[2] These principles have been published in the draft of ISO 9004 — guidance. Detailed commentary on the final version of ISO 9004 and 9001 — requirements will be published on our website (www.lean-service.com). This will be updated with successive reviews.

of view. After all, the customers will determine the longevity of the organisation.

Demand, value and flow. Rather than designing work in functional specialisms and managing the relationship between these, it is better to treat the design and management of work according to the principles of demand, value and flow: Demand — what are the nature of demands placed on the organisation by its customers? Value — what matters to customers in respect of the various demands? Flow — how does the "value work" flow through the organisation?

Integrating decision-making with work. To improve control, learning and hence performance improvement, it is essential to integrate decision-making with work.

Measures that relate to purpose, demonstrate capability and variation. Instead of using the more traditional measures associated with budget for managing, the integration of decision-making with work requires measures that can more clearly signal the quality and quantity of performance in process (flow) terms.

Co-operative attitude towards suppliers. Just as the above measures and methods are a prerequisite to improving internal performance, the same methods and measures are central to improving performance with suppliers — who should be treated as working in joint processes. Methods and measures are essential prerequisites to co-operation.

Learning ethos. The above principles together establish a learning ethos at all levels in an organisation. The consequence is greater control and improvement of operations.

These systems principles, if applied, lead an organisation to the same objective as ISO 9000. They are the practical means for achieving customer satisfaction and the continual improvement of the enterprise.

Interpretation and use of the eight principles

The Standard's eight principles — customer focus, leadership, involvement of people, process approach, systems approach to management, continual improvement, factual approach to decision-making and mutually beneficial supplier relationships — are like motherhood and apple pie: who could possibly argue against them? Clearly, while people and organisations might claim to subscribe to such principles, practices within an organisation may or may not be consistent with them. This is to make the distinction between espoused theory and theory-in-use.

In order to expand on a systems interpretation of the eight principles, we will introduce, en route, a further systems model (Purpose–Measures–Method). This model is at the heart of the Vanguard Standards; it provides a robust framework for managing and improving the work of an organisation.

We begin our discussion of the Standard's principles with the most important — a system approach to management.

System approach to management

> **"System approach to management — identifying, understanding and managing a system of interrelated processes for a given objective contributes to the effectiveness and efficiency of the organisation."**

The Standard says, "The quality management system of an organisation is an important part of the overall management system."

We disagree. The two are one. To achieve genuine and sustainable improvements in quality, an organisation must be understood and managed as a system. That is the job of management. It was the job envisaged by Admiral Rickover (see Chapter 1), and it is still the priority for management education. Throughout the Standard quality management is talked of as though it is one of a number of management disciplines. This will only get quality relegated to the quality department. Yet quality is made in the boardroom.

Systems thinking is at the heart of quality management and it represents a different and better way of designing and managing work. The managers of our organisations still need to learn how powerful this way of working is. This way of working is not additional to — it is better than. Rather than treat the quality management system as part of the management system, we would argue that managers should understand and manage their organisation *as* a system.

The Standard says, "Organisations should define their systems and the processes contained within them to enable the systems to be clearly understood, managed and improved." We agree. But the Standard does not provide useful guidance on how to do that. The Standard introduces a model for a "process approach to quality management" which is not unlike the Business Excellence or Baldrige models. It schematically identifies relationships between management responsibility, measurement, resources, product and/or services and the customer — and suggests that all of these relationships should be managed for continuous improvement. However, as we have seen with the Business Excellence and Baldrige models, this can lead to inappropriate action.[3] Our criticisms of the Excellence and Baldrige models are that they include too much "command and control" thinking in their content and encourage the wrong method for assessment — asking the user to create a score rather than understand the what and why of current performance as a system.

Developing a system picture. A picture of the organisation as a system is the pre-requisite for managing for sustained improvement. The elements of a system picture appear in Figures 9.2 to 9.4. These are elements of a model for which we have yet to find boundaries. It has been applied beneficially in commercial, non-profit and governmental organisations.

Three inter-related concepts help the construction of a systems view of an organisation: Purpose, measures and methods. These apply at the macro level — managing a customer-driven

---

[3] For a discussion of problems in interpretation and change management using the Excellence Model, see Appendix 1, Further Resources.

system — and at the micro level — managing an end-to-end customer-focused process. This simple but useful model will reappear as we discuss interpretation of the Standard.

Figure 9.1 Purpose, Measures, Methods — A Hierarchical Relationship

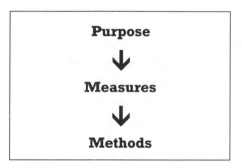

Purpose. The purpose of any commercial system is to get and keep customers.[4] Thus the first step in understanding the organisation as a system is to look "outside-in", to look at the organisation from the customers' point of view. The customers' view of an organisation can only be made up from the transactions they have with the organisation.

Figure 9.2 The Customers' View of the System

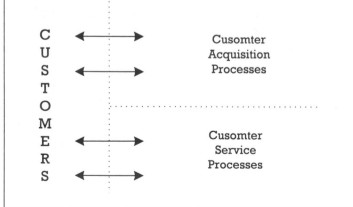

---

[4] These concepts work well for non-commercial organisations also, but the discussion of their application is beyond the scope of this book.

This is the starting place for building a system picture of an organisation — something that will help managers and all people manage it. It helps define the organisation's processes — they should be understood from the outside-in. Otherwise how could an organisation improve?

Having shown how a systems thinker would define processes, we move on to the next of the eight principles.

Process approach

"A desired result is achieved more efficiently when related resources and activities are managed as a process."

The Standard talks of process management in what we would describe as "engineering terms": "Any activity that receives and connects them to outputs can be considered as a process". This is unarguable, but it leads to any organisation activity being treated as a "process" worthy of managing and thus is misleading and unhelpful. By contrast, the approach we have outlined above always clarifies the importance of core processes — those that begin and end with the customer. In our experience, it is important to avoid an internal "customer-supplier" focus — all parties should be focused on the "end to end" process, the only focus for re-design and improvement.

Because ISO 9000 starts from a position where "quality management" is only one of a number of "management disciplines" it requires managers to "identify the processes needed for the quality management system" and "determine the sequence and interaction of these processes". This risks establishing a quality management bureaucracy. If managers take the position we take, quality management is synonymous with management and the model outlined (Figure 9.2) will help clarify the "processes needed" and their "interaction" (see also Figures 9.3 and 9.4. later).

In a significant departure from the previous versions of ISO 9000, the new Standard requires that managers "determine criteria and methods . . . to ensure the effective operation of . . . process" and *does not insist that processes are managed through procedures.*

Discussion documents preceding the new Standard explicitly acknowledged the historical problems of overdoing procedures. However, little guidance is offered in terms of any alternative, and the risk is that a procedures approach will continue.

We would advise managers to firstly address the following question: "Are the people who work in the process in control of their method(s)?" Procedures may help where they are known to be critical to performance, but they should not become the *raison d'etre*. The case studies conducted with Takaji Nishizawa showed how the "best" organisations avoided writing procedures; instead they had integrated basic flows within their quality manuals. Further, as Nishizawa points out (see Appendix), it is a mistake to have the wrong information in the work flow.

The historic emphasis on control on procedures was, effectively, to focus on conformance rather than performance. The emphasis on conformance has now shifted to an emphasis on consistency. The question is: Will this lead people in the direction of understanding capability (and variation), a systems approach, or will people interpret consistency as conformance?

Of course inspection of peoples' work with respect to conformance to procedures was and is the life-blood of the ISO 9000 community. Inspection begins with documentation. Here again we find that the new Standard implicitly warns against overdoing documentation ("The nature and extent of the documentation should support the needs of the organisation"). We would strongly support the view that documentation should be kept to a minimum and inspection should focus more on the work then on documents.

Having identified processes from the outside-in, the next step in building a system picture is to measure, so we turn to the Standard's principle concerning measurement:

Factual approach to decision making

"**Effective decisions are based on the logical and intuitive analysis of data and information.**"

The Standard states, "The organisation shall define, plan and implement measurement and monitoring activities needed to ensure conformity and achieve improvement". As noted above, the thrust of the traditional thinking about measurement was towards conformance; this is not the same as measurement for learning and improvement. Conformance is "go/no-go" thinking, it is "static" thinking. Improvement measures are concerned with capability and variation, they are, by contrast, concerned with "flow" thinking. With respect to variation, the Standard goes on to say, "This shall include the determination of the need for, and the use of, applicable methodologies including statistical techniques" but gives no guidance on how and where to apply such tools. People close to the review committees have told us that the UK committee specifically excluded any additions to ISO 9000:2000 that introduced the theory of variation. Yet this theory is central to understanding the theory of quality.

When discussing measures, the Standard now advises more than simply measures of conformance. Reading through the various examples of measures given in ISO 9004:2000; most managers are likely to feel overwhelmed. Worse, few managers will be able to distinguish the chaff from the wheat — many of the measures used in examples are not good system measures and could lead to sub-optimisation of performance.

However, the Standard says managers shall define their own measurement system, hence it is entirely feasible to do so from a systems perspective. If managers chose to, this is how they would proceed:

Measures: The second step in building a system picture is to measure, to establish measures of capability between the system and its customers — this tells you "what" but not "why".

Measures of the capability of customer acquisition processes tell you how and how well you get customers. Measures of the capability of service processes tell you how and how well you provide services (and products) to your customers.

Figure 9.3 Capability at the Points of the Transaction

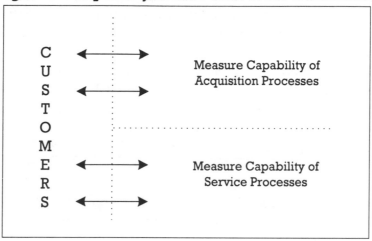

And from measures, managers should go to method:

Methods. To find out more about the "why" of performance, you have to look at the organisations processes. The core processes are, by definition, those that touch the customers. Their purpose is to create value for customers and the measures (above) should describe how well they do that. The purpose of any support process is to provide "value" to the core processes; and they should be measured that way.

Figure 9.4 Core and Support Processes

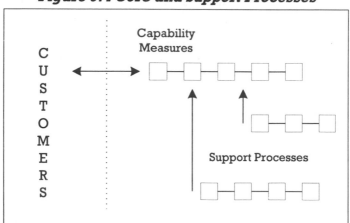

Working from measures to methods is important, for many things might affect performance in the system. What matters is finding out specifically what does affect performance and how.[5] This is made easier when measures of performance are established prior to looking at "how". By contrast, to look at method without first establishing performance — as ISO 9000 has done historically, by emphasising procedures over purpose — often leads to wasteful work. To think of processes as something that "transforms input into output" will lead to the wrong focus. Moving from "what" to "why" ensures that the focus is on learning rather than control.

The system picture being created is completely customer focused; now let us compare what has been built thus far with the next principle:

Customer focus

> **"Organisations depend on their customers and therefore should understand current and future customer needs, meet customer requirements and strive to exceed customer expectations."**

We have already noted the tendency amongst "command and control" thinkers to assume this means conducting customer surveys, we have also noted the waste associated with "how was it for you" data that traditional surveys often generate. Again, however, this principle, and its associated clauses could be interpreted from a systems view. The priorities are to know what matters to customers at each and every point of transaction and to know the nature of demands placed on the organisation by its customers. Both sets of data will be usable for improvement.

The data about customers should be used for action not reporting and, furthermore, the data need to be integrated with the work. The requirement for documented procedures for

---

[5] There are a variety of "system conditions" that can affect performance — structure, work design, measures, information and so on. It is the job of leaders to understand how their particular system conditions help or hinder performance improvement.

complaint handling should be loosely interpreted, and defended as such. Complaints procedures destroy the truth (see page 122) and create enormous amounts of waste. Any complaints procedure needs to say no more than "see the truth and do the right thing". The extent to which this would require documentation rather than just common sense governed by normal financial controls would depend on the complexity of the relationship with the customer.

The principles discussed thus far have led to a basic framework for understanding the what and why of current performance as a system. It is the leaders who should use this system picture to manage and improve their organisation. Thus we turn to the leadership principle:

Leadership

> **"Leaders establish unity of purpose, direction, and the internal environment of the organisation. They create the environment in which people can become fully involved in achieving the organisation's objectives."**

This is not a satisfactory expression of what is required from leaders. This will be interpreted as writing "visions" and "missions" — TC176 did so themselves and the same language appears in the Standard. Clearly leaders should be responsible for unity of purpose, but by what means? The Standard shows no change in its language about leadership; it describes leadership in "objective-setting" and "review" terms. This is to take a "command and control" perspective. The Standard also continues the practice of encouraging the appointment of a "management representative", something we would not condone as quality — performance improvement — is every leaders' job. We have found the best leaders to be in touch with their operations, leading learning — if leaders are learning their people do too. The work in developing a system picture discussed here is the work of top management. As their work progresses they learn for themselves how their traditional practices have actually caused sub-optimisation (ISO 9000 registration being only one cause).

The priority for all leaders is to understand how to act on their organisation as a system. This cannot be done in offices, it can only be done where the work is done. When leaders learn to do this work they effectively lead learning in the organisation and, consequentially, their people begin to learn and contribute to a far greater extent that is possible in a traditional, hierarchical "command and control" system. Which leads us to the next of the eight principles:

Involvement of people

> **"People at all levels are the essence of an organisation and their full involvement enables their abilities to be used for the organisation's benefit."**

There can be no argument with this sentiment. However it is the case that our most common organisation form, the mass production system, is designed to inhibit people's contribution. In an early draft of the new Standard, it said "attention should be given to empowerment of people when defining authority". Interestingly the word "empowerment" does not appear in the final draft. Instead, the words "to stimulate innovation" and "encourage the involvement of people" are used. Empowerment is a pre-occupation of command and control or mass production thinkers — they design systems that disempower people, notice the same and then do things to try to empower people. The answer, of course, is to change the system. When people who do the work have measures that relate to purpose in their hands such that they can work on method, empowerment, innovation and involvement follow.

The Standard uses terms that are familiar in a command and control environment. There is an emphasis on internal communications, generally emphasised as through the hierarchy. It uses the terms "competencies" and "recognition". "Competencies" has become a new buzz-word amongst HR professionals. Few ask the validation question: "If all people behaved this way, would the work work better?" Managers who are keen on incentives as a form of recognition are unaware of the extent to which incentives damage performance. These and other notions promulgated by this "involvement of people" principle in the Standard are no more than modern management speak — some recent "solutions" to a century-old problem. Similarly, and rather as the Excellence and Baldrige models do, the Standard encourages measuring staff satisfaction. Data from such surveys represent no more than symptoms. It is foolish and often counter-productive to act on them. To write these sorts of things in to your quality management system would be unwise.

The "full involvement" of people is dependent on how their work is designed and managed, not whether the organisation has recognition schemes, competency frameworks, staff surveys and so on. The systems approach is to integrate decision-making with work. The consequence is peoples' involvement follows naturally; people bring their brains to work which is an essential pre-requisite for improvement:

Continual improvement

"Continual improvement is a permanent objective of the organisation."

But the Standard says little or nothing about by what method. ISO 9004: 2000 is described as "guidelines for performance improvement", but we would say if you want to improve you need to look outside-in, define and measure you processes in customer terms, ensure process measures are end-to-end and in the hands of people doing the work and then lead this system. This is not the way that 9001 and 9004 describe method. To the extent that the Standard does describe a method, it concentrates on notions of "plan", "target", "review" and so on - all traditional, command and control concepts. However, there is nothing to prevent the user interpreting continual improvement in systems terms.

The integration of decision-making with work, employing measures related to purpose has a profound effect on people. They become engaged. Similarly, the same philosophy applies to the way work is done with suppliers:

Mutually beneficial supplier relationships

> **"Mutually beneficial relationships between the organisation and its suppliers enhance the ability of both organisations to create value."**

But again, little is said about method. The clauses on the treatment of suppliers remain very similar to the previous versions of the Standard: "The organisation shall control its purchasing processes . . . and . . . evaluate and select suppliers . . . ." While 9004 talks about partnerships with suppliers, there is little advice beyond joint identification of the customers and each parties needs. The starting-place for partnerships is method – and to get there you have to be clear about what joint purpose you serve. If purpose and measures can be agreed, the parties can get to work on method. It should be sufficient to record that suppliers have been established as partners because they share the same attitude. No requirement for suppliers to register to ISO 9000 should be necessary or even considered positive.

Is ISO 9000: 2000 an improvement?

While much of the content in the new Standard represents a significant shift towards "improvement" much of the philosophy within the Standard has remained largely the same. While there is the beginnings of systems terminology, there remain significant amounts of non-systems content. The Standard lacks integrity. It is contradictory, confusing and, worst of all, more demanding.

Too much of the thinking within the new Standard remains rooted in conformance and inspection thinking. Although it makes an attempt, it has yet to make the leap to improvement versus purpose (systems) thinking. However, for the first time in its history, ISO 9000 now provides scope for a systems interpretation.

Where do we go from here?

Managers may take the opportunity provided by the review of ISO 9000 to de-register their organisations. The ready excuse is the expansion of the requirements beyond what they currently have to do; there will be debates about whether this will be worth the effort. Moreover, managers may, quite rightly, doubt the ability of assessors to work with the new Standard.

Managers may find themselves another excuse for de-registration. The new Standard's closeness to the Business Excellence and Baldrige Models, and encouragement of self-assessment, may lead managers to decide to invest their energy in only one model for self-assessment. The potential merging of ISO 9000 with the Excellence and Baldrige models will repeat the same weaknesses in terms of content and method. It will not result in better management of our organisations.

The only thing that has maintained ISO 9000 has been marketplace coercion. Coercion is still the only pillar holding it up and is likely to weaken as all interested parties reflect on the revision. It is not insignificant that the UK's President of the Board of Trade remarked on radio that "the logos seen on vehicles are of little guarantee of service or quality". There is no doubt in our minds that he was referring to ISO 9000.

In short, the new Standard is more complex, has more requirements and will demand different qualities amongst assessors. It will be understandable if managers and organisations choose to take this opportunity to walk away. The only question is, will marketplace coercion keep ISO 9000 alive?

Our advice remains the same

Our advice is unequivocal. ISO 9000 registration should be avoided. In our work with organisations we continue to come across examples like those described in this book. Registration to ISO 9000 makes organisations do things that make them worse and it prevents them doing things they should do to make them better. Despite the revision's attempt to improve the theory and practice of ISO 9000 registration, inevitably — because of the players — the result does not shift far enough.

However, the fact is that marketplace coercion continues to cause a growth in registrations. Because of this we advise that if you do feel unable to say no to ISO 9000 registration, you should use the Vanguard Standards to guide your interpretation and use. The Vanguard Standards were developed in conjunction with clients who felt they needed — because of marketplace coercion — to be registered to ISO 9000 but who wanted to take a systems approach to the design and management of their work.

The Vanguard Standards are published at www.lean-service.com. They are available free of charge and will be updated as the ISO 9000 Standards are reviewed.

Appendix

TAKAJI NISHIZAWA'S EIGHT PRINCIPLES FOR ISO 9000 IMPLEMENTATION

Following his visit to the UK to study ISO 9000 in practice, Takaji Nishizawa published the following advice to Japanese users of ISO 9000:

1. Absorb management procedures into a quality manual.

As we saw with the best of the case studies (Chapter 6) the quality management system and management procedures should be integrated in to the same document. Then point two follows:

2. The quality manual should not need a revision history of each page and distribution control. One page of revision history for a manual is enough.

The usual requirement for revision history of each page and distribution control is caused by the practice of having wasteful document control and many copies of the quality manual. There is only a need for one quality manual. It should represent the whole system and should not be required to be held in all locations, for only specific information about things that change are needed in the work place (see point 7 below).

As the object is to look at the organisation through one set of eyes, point 3 follows:

3. Integrate ISO 9000 with the production control system.

Production control deals with quality, schedule and costs altogether. The methods of production and production improvement should be part of the same overall system and hence the methods and measures associated with production (or service) should be included in the single quality manual. Information relevant to particular quality characteristics should be made available separately (see 6 (b) below).

4. Maintain a document numbering system only for customer drawing numbers.

This is the only case where documents need to be controlled. In order to access necessary documents, we should use their name, not an abstract numbering system.

5. Separate management standards from technical ones.

The management system is not the same as the technical system. The technical data (except 'type 'a' – see point 7 below) are always applicable to the specifics being made or provided and should thus be available to the workforce (see point 7).

6. Classify documents into the following two types, to make the total number of documents minimal:

Type "a" — documents which a manager or operator uses repeatedly, for example the quality manual, operating procedures for machines and equipment, etc. Type "b" — documents which a manager or operator uses specifically for each job, for example order sheets, drawings, etc.

Type "a" documents should be used for training new staff and managers. They should not be needed on the working sites as notices or job aids; these documents should be known and understood by all workers and managers. If you have a driving licence, you don't make use of a driving manual. If you read a driving manual while driving it is dangerous.

Type "b" documents should be used specifically — to ensure quality is made in the process(es). They should be distributed when they are needed in the process, according to the production control system. Even if you have a driving licence, you will need a map if you go to an unfamiliar location.

7. Treat process design as a part of design control.

Design of products or services should include consideration of process design. For example, ease of manufacturing, ease of assembly, ease of installation and ease of service. In this way, quality is designed in to processes.

8. In corrective action and preventive action, use the techniques used in the Toyota system. For example:

- Three "gen" principles:
  ◊ Gen Ba — go straight to the workplace when a problem occurs.
  ◊ Gen Butsu — Look at and examine the actual defect(s); they tell the truth.
  ◊ Gen Jitsu — combine the observed facts with a practical hypothesis. Now you are in a position to take action with prediction of the consequences.
- Five Why's — when a problem occurs, ask "why" five times.
- The Three M's:
  ◊ Muda — wastefulness, eliminate surplus
  ◊ Mura — unequalness, make level or balanced
  ◊ Muri — strain, reduce "struggle" (make things easier to carry)
- Pokayoke — mistake-proofing: preventing processes from proceeding with defects.
- The Five S's:
  ◊ Seiri — instant disposal of things which are unnecessary
  ◊ Seiton — placing things in order
  ◊ Seiketsu — make the workplace clean
  ◊ Seiso — do clean work positively
  ◊ Shitsuke — be well-mannered.

INDEX